A Legacy Transformed

A Legacy Transformed

THE STORY OF HPER AND THE BIRTH OF THE
SCHOOL OF PUBLIC HEALTH-BLOOMINGTON

Mohammad R. Torabi & Barbara A. Hawkins

With the Assistance of David M. Skirvin

Indiana University Press | Bloomington and Indianapolis

This book is a publication of

Indiana University Press
Office of Scholarly Publishing
Herman B Wells Library 350
1320 East 10th Street
Bloomington, Indiana 47405 USA
iupress.indiana.edu

Manufactured by Pacom in South Korea.

The paper used in this publication meets the
minimum requirements of the American
National Standard for Information Sciences—
Permanence of Paper for Printed Library
Materials, ANSI Z39.48-1992.

Cataloging information is available from the
Library of Congress.

ISBN 978-0-253-01928-8 (cloth)

1 2 3 4 5 20 19 18 17 16 15

Dedicated to the alumni, staff, university administrators, trustees, and faculty members who contributed to the legacy of excellence and success that throughout its history characterized the former School of Health, Physical Education, and Recreation, which served as a solid foundation for building an already prominent School of Public Health–Bloomington!

What you seek is seeking you.

—Rumi

Patience is not sitting and waiting, it is foreseeing.
It is looking at the thorn and seeing the rose,
looking at the night and seeing the day.
Lovers are patient and know that the moon
needs time to become full.

—Rumi

Contents

President's Message

THE SCHOOL OF HEALTH, PHYSICAL EDUCATION, AND RECREATION
has indeed had a rich history on the Bloomington campus. Included in that
rich history are many endeavors that have greatly enhanced the health of
Indiana's citizens. As we reimagine Indiana University for the twenty-first
century, the School of Public Health–Bloomington—bolstered by epidemiology and other highly effective tools of public health, and by its outstanding faculty, students, and staff—will help lead the way in cultivating a
healthier citizenry in Indiana and across the nation.

Michael McRobbie
President, Indiana University

A Message from the Provost

THE SCHOOL OF PUBLIC HEALTH HELPS FULFILL A KEY MISSION
of this campus: to improve the health of the state, and the nation, by
building true excellence in health research and education. The multi-
disciplinary nature of Indiana University Bloomington, coupled with
our unmatched technological capabilities, has inspired collaborations
that are leading to innovative approaches to some of the most pressing
public health issues. As faculty researchers and new generations of
health professionals take their mission into the world, we can all look
toward a healthier future.

Lauren Robel
Provost and Executive Vice President
Indiana University

Dean Mohammad Torabi with son and Herman B Wells, April 26, 1998. Courtesy of IU Archives (P0053089).

To the Reader

MORE THAN THREE YEARS AGO, I ENVISIONED WRITING A book that would synthesize almost seven decades of history of the School of Health, Physical Education, and Recreation and its successful transition to a forward-looking and prominent School of Public Health–Bloomington. The school's legacy of excellence in making positive differences in the health and well-being of individuals and communities at local, national, and global levels is due to the hard work of former and current faculty, loyal alumni, dedicated staff, and progressive administrators of Indiana University Bloomington. In particular, I want to thank the ongoing and visionary support of President Michael McRobbie, Provost Lauren Robel, and former University leaders Karen Hansen and Ed Marshall.

The school's overall mission has been the prevention of disease, promotion of health, and enhancement of quality of life. For me, the school is an embodiment of the ancient Persian saying "Alaje vaghae ghabl as voughou bayad kard" (Prevention is the ultimate cure). The school always has been ahead of its time in recognizing that the prevention of suffering and premature death and the enhancement of health and quality of life are very much related to lifestyle. It is remarkable that about seven decades ago, our former colleagues correctly predicted that physical activity, tobacco prevention, proper nutrition, healthy lifestyles, and sound public policy would be critical components in combating the leading causes of death in the twenty-first century. Today, the school continues to address ways to combat the chronic conditions that affect society, namely, heart disease, cancer, stroke, diabetes, and obesity.

My hope is that this book, even with its many oversights and shortcomings, will help forge a link between our glorious past and our commitment to forging a better, healthier future for people throughout the world. While this book provides only a glance at our school's legacy, we welcome your comments and feedback as we continually strive to document the school's activities. Honoring the past and anticipating the future always will be a focus of our publications and communications. Your input will guide our efforts.

As the Founding Dean of the School of Public Health–Bloomington, I would like to offer my heartfelt thanks to my coauthor, the extraordinary researcher Barbara Hawkins, whose passion for objectivity, loyalty to our school, and dedication to making a difference have exceeded my wildest expectations. I also am appreciative of the assistance rendered by Assistant Dean David Skirvin.

Simply put, I am fortunate to have had the honor of following in the footsteps of many past leaders who laid down a solid foundation for me to build upon. I pledge to sustain excellence in all that the school does to ensure a future that builds on the legacy of the past. I often proudly remind my colleagues and friends that I have had the honor of leading and serving two schools: the School of Health, Physical Education, and Recreation, and the School of Public Health–Bloomington.

Mohammad R. Torabi
Founding Dean and Chancellor's Professor
Indiana University School of Public Health–Bloomington

Preface

WILLIAM LOWE BRYAN, INDIANA UNIVERSITY'S TENTH AND
longest-serving president (1902–1937), embraced a philosophy
that was instrumental to the development of the professional
schools at the university. It was a philosophy rooted in the belief
that "every occupation arose in response to a deep social need
for a certain service, performed by generations of men forming a
sort of brotherhood or guild, whose history extends back to the
farthest antiquity."

There are three important ideas expressed here. First, any
service that is provided is in response to a social need. Second,
people will be attracted to providing service as a means of
making a living. Finally, occupations will emerge and the people
who assume these occupations will form a guild. Professions
are born of this process, and President Bryan envisioned that
professional schools would provide the foundation upon which
the university would grow.

In one of his early addresses, Bryan spoke of the role of
education in preparing occupations: "Here, as I think, is the
program for our educational system—to make plain highways
from every corner of the State to every occupation which history
has proved good."

Bryan steadfastly expected that the university would grow
because it would cultivate education for the occupations that
society needed. As a consequence, the university established
schools of law, medicine, and business, which were then followed by schools of education, music, nursing, and other disciplines. The establishment of professional schools has continued
into the twenty-first century.

During Bryan's era, America was challenged by a particular
set of social needs that were the byproducts of rapid urbanization, industrialization, population growth, the Great Depression, and World War I. Occupations associated with health and
safety, physical fitness and education, and recreation and parks
arose in response to those needs. At Indiana University (IU),
professional education programs in these areas emerged in various forms throughout this period. Growth in these programs

William Lowe Bryan. Photograph from the 1898 Arbutus yearbook. Courtesy of IU Archives (P0043954).

was such that by the mid-1930s professional education was dispersed across the IU campus. It became evident that the programs were in need of consolidation under one administration, but with the coming of World War II administrators delayed taking such action.

When the war ended, the university moved forward with plans for a School of Health, Physical Education, and Recreation (HPER). The school was approved by the Board of Trustees in the fall of 1945 and officially opened on July 1, 1946. It was a significant accomplishment. The university had taken a progressive and bold move to found a school exclusively devoted to matters of health and safety, physical education, and recreation and parks, especially as the nation was recovering from World War II and the lingering poverty of the Great Depression.

The history of HPER is rich and revealing.* This book provides the reader with a brief portrait of some of the people, events, and accomplishments that reflect the character and legacy of the school from its founding, subsequent evolution, and final transition to the IU School of Public Health–Bloomington in 2012. Throughout this period, Indiana University provided an environment for the HPER professions to grow and flourish. As the health needs and conditions of Americans changed throughout the twentieth century and into the twenty-first century, so did the education for HPER professions. The school was instrumental in leading the development in professional preparation, research, and service that responded to social needs and changes. This book leads the reader through the school's journey of development, growth, and change—a journey that culminates at a critical juncture in its history. It is no small consequence that Indiana University responded to the

*A Chronological History of the School of Health, Physical Education, and Recreation, which I prepared, is available at the University Archives and the Dean's Office in the School of Public Health–Bloomington.

local and global community needs, trends, and social conditions of twenty-first-century America by embracing public health as the school's new platform for innovation and growth.

The journey begins by framing the early roots for what would become the foundation for the school. These roots focus the reader's attention on health as achieved through physical training and sport. By the time the school was operational in 1946, the perils that affected personal health in America were being shaped by social conditions related to war, poverty, industrialization, urbanization, and rapid population growth. Health and safety education, physical fitness through education, and healthful recreation were seen as appropriate responses to the conditions of the times. An educated professional workforce was embraced to meet the need for high-quality programs and services. The HPER professions specialized and matured throughout the twentieth century as American life advanced to a postindustrial society of relative affluence. By the turn of the century, new social needs and problems associated with chronic disease, unhealthy lifestyles, and community decline emerged, and the response to these changes, as in the past, is the central theme of the school's recent history. This book interprets the history of the School of HPER, but it is in no way a comprehensive account. While we have been selective in our approach, we hope the book will provide the reader with an appreciation of the historical importance of the school to Indiana University, the state, and the nation. We also hope that it will provide the framework for understanding the significance of the school's evolution into a School of Public Health.

Barbara A. Hawkins
Professor Emeritus
Indiana University School of Public Health–Bloomington

Acknowledgments

WE ARE INDEBTED TO THE FOLLOWING PEOPLE FOR THEIR ASSISTANCE and contributions to this publication, as well as to the past, present, and future of the Indiana University School of Public Health–Bloomington.

DONALD LUDWIG, Professor Emeritus of Health and Safety Education

CLINT STRONG, Professor Emeritus of Kinesiology

EDNA MUNRO, Professor Emeritus of Physical Education for Women

BRADLEY COOK, Curator of Photographs, Office of University Archives & Records Management, Indiana University

BOB SLOAN, Editor-in-Chief, Indiana University Press

All former deans and university administrators who provided instrumental leadership and support to the school throughout its history

Panorama of Old Crescent, 1908.
From left to right: Franklin Hall, Student Building, Maxwell Hall, Carpenter Shop (barely visible as a long white-looking rectangle), Owen Hall, Assembly Hall (with construction progressing on Well House between viewer and Assembly Hall), Wylie Hall, Kirkwood Hall, and Lindley Hall. Photograph by City Book & News Company. Courtesy of IU Archives (P0022486).

ALL   OWEN HALL.

Y. BLOOMINGTON, INDIANA.   WYLIE HALL.   KIRKWOOD HALL.   H AND COLORED   SCIENCE HALL.

Athenaeum, c. 1945. Courtesy of Athenaeum Foundation,
http://www.athenaeumfoundation.org/about-the-A/history/.

Roots

THE ROOTS OF THE SCHOOL OF HEALTH, PHYSICAL EDUCATION, and Recreation extend back into the nineteenth century. In the early to mid-1800s, gymnastics as a form of training for a sound mind and sound body was introduced in the United States. The German Turner movement, whose members were known as the "Turnvereins" for the "athletic clubs" they established, was one of a number of gymnastic systems introduced into America by German immigrants. Gymnastics had become so popular by the 1860s that the first school for instruction in physical training, the Normal College of the American Gymnastic Union, was established in New York City. By 1907, the Normal College had moved to Indianapolis. (It would merge with Indiana University in 1940–1941.) For Indiana University it was a fortuitous move. Physical training activities had already begun to appear on the IU campus with the establishment of separate gymnasia for men and women in the early 1890s. A relationship between the Normal College and the university blossomed. During the 1940–1941 school year, the college merged with IU, acquiring the rather unwieldy name of the Normal College of the American Gymnastic Union of Indiana University.

When the School of HPER was formally established in 1946, the college became administratively part of the newly established school. During the time that the Normal College was part of HPER, students spent two years in the Normal College and then two years on the Indiana University campus to complete their degrees. The Normal College remained a unit in the School of HPER until 1970, when it became an entity of Indiana University-Purdue University Indianapolis (IUPUI). By the academic year 1973–1974, the Normal College had become the School of Physical Education at IUPUI, renamed the School of Physical Education and Tourism Management in 2002.

A second significant motivating force behind programs for health, physical training, and recreation can be found in the development of sports and athletics on American college campuses. Baseball became IU's first official athletic activity in 1867, followed by men's football in 1886.

(overleaf, left) Normal College of the American Gymnastic Union, November 18, 1941. Photograph by the Athletic Department. Courtesy of IU Archives (P0035788).

(overleaf, right) Normal College faculty, November 3, 1941. From left to right: Emil Rinsch, Randolph Schreiber, H. Steichmann, and Clara Hester. Photograph by the Athletic Department. Courtesy of IU Archives (P0035651).

In the mid-1800s, intercollegiate sports began to appear; started in 1898, men's basketball played its first official intercollegiate games in 1901. Sports on the IU campus became an increasingly important part of student life, as can be seen with the offering of basketball to women as early as 1901 by the Department of Physical Training for Women. Indiana University joined the Western Conference for intercollegiate athletics in 1899, which was referred to as the Big Ten Conference as early as 1917.

The importance of the emergence of athletics on the Indiana University campus was the differentiation of athletics as competitive sport from physical training/education for a healthy mind and body. In the first quarter of the twentieth century, both athletics and physical training gave rise to courses and programs that eventually fashioned the School of HPER.

THE FORMATIVE YEARS of organized instruction in health and physical education, from the early gymnasia through to the founding of the IU School of HPER, were times of tremendous growth in the United States, with increasing population, rapid urbanization, and expanding wealth—checked during the Great Depression by a period of abject poverty and disease for many, and then a world war and its aftereffects.

The Progressives, who lend their name to the era between 1890 and 1920, were modernizers who believed in science, technology, expertise, and education as comprehensive solutions to society's problems. For them, education was instrumental to social change, especially concerning the transformation of society under the forces of urbanization, industrialization, population expansion, and war. Jobs in health, physical education, and recreation were becoming increasingly professionalized, in many cases requiring college training. At the same time, the societal need for healthy citizens in burgeoning cities where population density and rapid industrialization threatened

School and Community Health Education

The first School and Community Health Workshop was conducted in 1944 under the direction of Willard W. Patty, Professor of Education, Director of the Physical Welfare Training Department, and Director of the Normal College. Patty worked in collaboration with Frank S. Stafford, Director of the Division of Health and Physical Education, Indiana State Board of Health and State Director of Physical Fitness, Indiana State Defense Council. The workshop was the earliest cooperative education program that directly addressed health concerns and problems in Indiana. War had heightened concern over local health problems such as hygiene, sanitation, and communicable disease control. The situation provided the impetus for the university to assist school administrators, health educators, and public health personnel in finding solutions through training, program development, evaluation, and health education. It was significant that this highly popular and well-attended workshop continued for more than twenty years of annual offering. The workshop embodied Indiana University's early leadership in public health education.

personal well-being was mirrored on college campuses with the recognition of the need for healthy and physically fit students.

Indiana University President David Starr Jordan, who was a strong advocate of the student-athlete and healthful lifestyles for students, recommended the construction of gymnasia for both women and men in the 1890s. He appointed directors of the Women's and Men's Gymnasia and established an Athletic Committee. James Lilly Zink was appointed Director of the Men's

Malcolm "Mac" McDonald, the father of baseball at IU, c. 1867. Photograph from the 1940 Arbutus yearbook, page 7. Courtesy of IU Archives (P0021446).

IU Athletic Logo, 1899. Image from the Section page for Athletics in the 1899 Arbutus yearbook, page 135. Art by Vawter. Courtesy of IU Archives (P0022792).

1910 Football
Mann, Trainer; Lindley, Lewis, King, Winter
Messick   Hatfield, Kimble, Gill, Davis
Roberts, Dutter, Berndt (Capt), Hoover, Cunningham, Sheldon, (coach)

IU Football team, 1910. Not one touchdown was scored against this football team. They lost one game, to Illinois, by a score of 0-3. Front row, from left to right: George M. "Mose" "Lucky Jim" Roberts, Homer Williams "Dut" Dutter, Arthur Henry "Cotton" Berndt, Walter "Hoov" Hoover, Ashel "Heze" "Cunny" "Nig" Cunningham, Coach James "Jimmy" Sheldon. Middle row, from left to right: Allen George "Feeb" Messick, "Hatter" Hatfield, Frank "Ag" "Kim" Kimble, Andy Gill, Paul Yakey "Davy" Davis. Back row, from left to right: Trainer Mann, Frank Irvin "Monk" Lindley, Walter O. "Lewie" Lewis, Harold A. "Kingy" King, Olice "Alice" Winter. Not pictured is Lloyd Otterbein Sholty. Courtesy of IU Archives (P0053063).

IU's first varsity basketball team, 1900–1901. Front row (seated), from left to right: Phelps Darby, Ernest Strange, Jay Fitzgerald, Alvah J. Rucker. Back row (standing), from left to right: Thomas Records, Charles Unnewehr, Ernest Walker, Coach James H. Horne. Photograph from the 1901 Arbutus yearbook. Courtesy of IU Archives (P0020320).

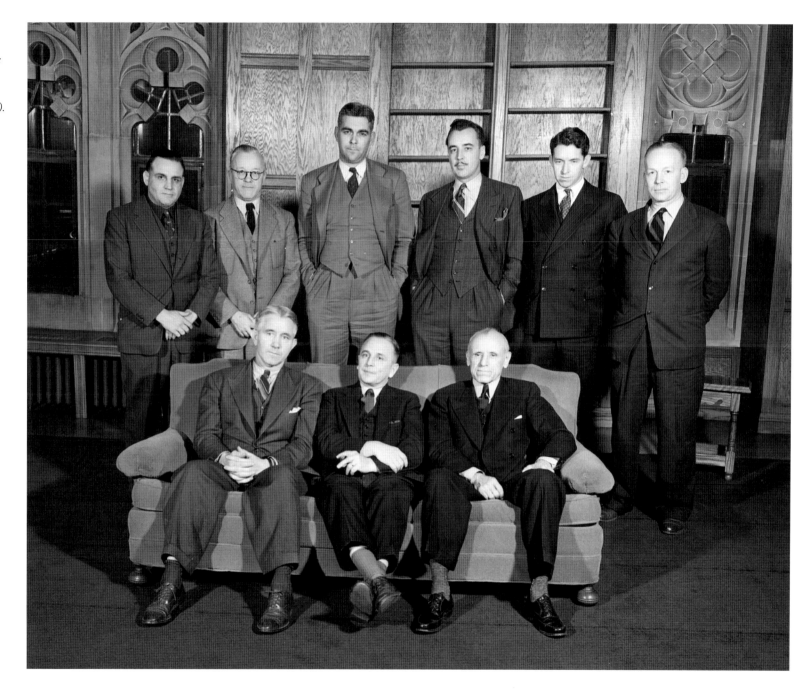

IU Athletic Coaches, February 3, 1942. Front row, from left to right: "Bo" McMillin (Football), Hugh Willis (Golf), Zora Clevenger (Athletic Director). Back row, from left to right: William "Billy" Thom (Wrestling), "Billy" Hayes (Track), "Branch" McCracken (Basketball), Robert Royer (Swimming), Ralph Collins (Tennis), Paul "Pooch" Harrell (Baseball). Photograph by the Athletic Department. Courtesy of IU Archives (P0043967).

Gymnasium, and Harriet Saunderson became the first Director of the Women's Gymnasium. Julietta Maxwell followed Saunderson as Director and Instructor of the Women's Gymnasium of Physical Training. Maxwell, daughter of David Maxwell, then the president of the IU Board of Trustees, came to the position after teaching for two years at Coats College in Terre Haute. Variously known as class work, practice, and service, the first elective physical education program was initiated in 1897. The 1890s saw such growth in both the women's and the men's programs that courses in theory and practice, physiology, and hygiene had appeared in the university catalogue by the turn of the century.

Enrollment at IU had rapidly increased, from around 350 students in 1890 to 600 students in 1900. Some tension existed about the expansion of the university in response to the needs of the people of Indiana and the management of resources. While new programs and schools would soon be created to meet those needs, it is significant that physical education/training and hygiene were already established programs in the university. Physical training for men and women, the elective program of sports and activities, and competitive athletics were staples of campus life.

The Student Building, completed in 1906, became the home of the women's physical education department for many years, with greatly expanded facilities including a gymnasium, a locker room, a swimming pool with adjoining showers, and three tub baths. With the expanded facilities and course offerings, the first matron to serve student needs was hired. At the time, Dunn Meadow was used for women's training and course work. As noted by Edna Munro in her history of the department,

"Distractions abounded for men who were passing by and were captivated by women in sporting attire and performing physical acts associated with sport and training. Of course, the men had their own separate facilities and faculty."

Throughout the 1930s, IU felt the impact of the Great Depression, with all the programs associated with health, physical education, and recreation confronting many challenges. Financial support was lean, facilities were in need of modernization, and new faculty members were needed for the different academic programs. Curricula in physical education (men and women separately), coaching, health, hygiene, recreation, safety, and public health nursing were spread around campus, some being housed in the College of Arts and Sciences and others, like the Department of Physical Welfare Training, in the School of Education. Athletics continued to be a mainstay of campus life, with coaches heavily engaged in both coaching and teaching responsibilities. By the late 1930s, academic programs were so dispersed that the need for a single administrative unit became evident.

World War II not only slowed the movement toward a unified school but also sparked the development of a massive physical fitness program on campus in 1942. Herman T. Briscoe, Dean of Facilities, proposed a program of physical training for men students who would be called early in the summer for military service. The work was offered daily between the hours 4:30 p.m. to 6:00 p.m. As a consequence of World War II, all undergraduate men and women were required to take fitness work. Classes were held from 7:00 a.m. to 6:00 p.m. including the noon hour.

(facing) Student Building, c. 1926. Photograph by Sinclair Studio, Bloomington, Indiana. Courtesy of IU Archives (P0023146).

A Tribute to Herman B Wells

Herman B Wells, November 1947. Photograph by IU Photographic Services. Courtesy of IU Archives (P0030164).

As the president of a large public university, Herman B Wells understood the importance of a sound body and sound mind for each and every university student. Aware of the growing need for educated professionals in the areas of health, physical education, and recreation, Wells saw an opportunity for Indiana University to lead the nation in these fields. His vision built upon the foundation provided by President William Lowe Bryan, who ardently believed that the university would grow and become strong by educating professionals to help address the country's needs.

Herman B Wells' leadership and acts shaped the School of HPER and Indiana University. President Wells was a student and teacher of commerce and economics, but he was also a hearty participant in the pleasures of life. Hardly a trip was taken wherein he did not find and visit an antique shop. His passion for antiques was legendary and clearly spoke to the pleasures that filled his leisure. His pursuits underscored the importance of physical activity, such as swimming, driving in the country, the cultural arts, reveling at his Brown County cabin, or simply walking across campus on a daily basis.

We could say that he promoted health, physical education, and recreation because these disciplines were clearly instrumental to any citizen's healthy life, or that he did so because he lived his life so fully. In any event, the School of HPER was founded, grew, and became a national leader because Wells recognized the need for such a school, seized the opportunity to create it, and then promoted all that it represented.

One of the first gifts that Wells accepted as the president of the university was the deed to the Bradford Woods recreational site. Bradford Woods serves as an excellent example of both his visionary leadership and his entrepreneurial nature. Wells championed the development of the site and sought to turn it into the exceptional success that it is today. Likewise, he was intimately involved in the development of athletics as a vibrant aspect of student life on campus.

James Capshew, Wells' biographer, notes, "Herman B Wells continues to loom large on campus and in Bloomington as a whole. Wells' singular role in transforming what was once a middling small-town university into a world-class institution has firmly cemented his nearly mythic status as IU's greatest leader." In the same interview for *Bloom* magazine, Capshew aptly portrayed why Wells was so critical to the success of the School of HPER.

There were several facets of Wells' presidential style. On the one hand . . . he believed that less administration is better and that the university should hire the best possible faculty and leave them to do their jobs. He didn't have much in terms of money or resources to offer the new faculty he'd recruited, but Wells excelled in selling the idea that they'd work together for the renaissance of the university. So in one sense Wells' approach as president was putting the right people in place and enabling them to excel.

(facing) Swimming Pool in Student Building, c. 1939. Photograph by IU Photographic Services. Courtesy of IU Archives (P0030920).

For President Wells everyone, from dean to groundskeeper, was an important member of the IU community. He had an open door, open heart, and time to attend special occasions. He never forgot a name and always made you feel like you mattered, that you were important. He led by example, and all who had the chance to meet him were continually reminded of how lucky the university and the people who comprised it were. While President Wells appraised his life as one filled with great luck, many who have had splendid careers at Indiana University also feel that they have been exceptionally lucky due in no small part to his impact on the university. In this small space, tribute is paid to President Herman B Wells, who likely would be most pleased with the School of HPER's evolution into the Indiana University School of Public Health–Bloomington.

Herman B Wells receives deed to Bradford property.
Courtesy of IU Archives (P0053088).

BY 1944, WILLARD WALTER PATTY (fondly referred to as W. W. Patty), the head of the Normal College and Director of the Department of Physical Welfare Training on the Bloomington campus, had become discouraged about the apparent inertia toward establishing an autonomous school. As a result he persisted in urging the administration to move forward with establishing the School of HPER. Subsequently, University President Herman B Wells was proactive in facilitating the approval of the school by conducting a series of confidential correspondences to solicit input regarding the proposed school and its name. He sought input from Vice President and Treasurer Ward Gray Biddle; Athletic Director Zora Clevenger; E. Ross Bartley from the IU News Bureau; W. W. Patty; Henry Lester Smith, Dean of the School of Education; Herman Briscoe, Vice President and Dean of the Faculties; and Bernard W. Miller, Executive Secretary of the American Association for Health, Physical Education, and Recreation.

Looking for models for the proposed school, President Wells pointed out that Stanford University had organized a school of health that also included public health and medicine. He also noted that the University of Illinois had a school of physical education, but that it did not include all that was proposed for the new school at IU. Wells was concerned about possible confusion with public health, a discipline that was typically situated in medical schools. He noted that "physical welfare" was nomenclature that did not fully embrace all the

*Willard W. Patty, March 1941.
Photograph from the 1941
Arbutus yearbook, page 31.
Photograph by IU Photographic
Services. Courtesy of IU Archives
(P0034440).*

Degrees and Programs of the School

On July 13, 1946, the Board of Trustees approved Dean Patty's proposal for all the degree programs in the new School of HPER. Faculty members had much input for the Bachelor of Science and Master of Science degrees, but Dean Patty designed the director and doctoral degrees with assistance from Marjorie Phillips and Karl Bookwalter.

Degrees granted by the School of HPER as authorized by the IU Board of Trustees were:

FOUR-YEAR CURRICULUM

Bachelor of Science in Health and Safety

Bachelor of Science in Physical Education

Bachelor of Science in Recreation

SIX-YEAR CURRICULUM

Director of Health and Safety

Director of Physical Education

Director of Recreation

FIVE-YEAR CURRICULUM

Master of Science in Health and Safety

Master of Science in Physical Education

Master of Science in Recreation

SEVEN-YEAR CURRICULUM

Doctor of Health and Safety

Doctor of Physical Education

Doctor of Recreation

Additionally, the Board of Trustees approved the establishment of a Bureau of Service and Research. The bureau had the following functions:

- To develop the professional leadership of the school in the state and nation.
- To integrate the administration and promotion of professional research, survey, and advisory services of staff members to state and local school systems, park boards, and other community organizations in fields of Health, Physical Education, Athletics, and Recreation.
- To develop in a central place special equipment, expert research assistance, and special research references for faculty, graduate students, and workers in the field.
- To develop, if desirable, permanent exhibits in fields of Health, Safety, Physical Education, Athletics and Sports, and Recreation.
- To secure consignments of standard tests and similar materials in the various fields of the school to be sold.

fields proposed for the new school, including the mental and social areas.

Regarding the school name, Vice President Biddle was in favor of a shorter title. Ross Bartley had strong opinions about the inclusion of "health," because he felt it was in conflict with a School of Public Health, nor did he support "recreation," based on his belief that it would be the "subject of campus jokes innumerable." Bartley simply wanted a School of Physical Education. As would be expected, W. W. Patty thought the proposal was "perfect in plan and title." Dean Smith thought that courses related to the preparation of teachers should remain with the School of Education. Herman Briscoe favored leaving out "health" and "safety"; he noted that nursing education and public health nursing did not want to be included in the new school. Briscoe preferred the name School of Physical Welfare and Recreation. Dr. Ben Miller (IU alumnus and former IU faculty member, and at the time Executive Director of the American Alliance for Health, Physical Education, and Recreation) provided the most extensive and compelling argument for a School of Health, Physical Education, and Recreation. The essence of his argument was that the title was consistent with the national association and many state associations that represented the professional fields that were to form the new school.

What ensued is history, as they say. At the meeting of the Board of Trustees on September 20, 1945, President Wells recommended the establishment of a School of Health, Physical Education, and Recreation at Indiana University and the board so approved. Wells was authorized to negotiate for a dean. At the Board of Trustees meeting on May 20, 1946, President Wells recommended W. W. Patty, and on June 13, 1946, Wells reported to the trustees that Patty had accepted the appointment. The school became officially established and operational on July 1, 1946.

BY THE END OF AN ERA spanning 1890–1946, Indiana University had unmistakably affirmed its commitment to a physically fit and healthy student body, and to the provision of trained professionals in fields concerned with health, physical education, and recreation. It was clear from its early roots that the school evolved on the shoulders of progressive, spirited, and visionary leaders who believed unwaveringly in the promotion of personal health, fitness, well-being, and quality of life through the professions served by the school.

1890

The program Physical Training for Women traces its beginnings to a gymnasium that was housed in Wylie Hall; Harriet Saunderson is appointed Director of the Women's Gymnasium.

Wylie Hall, c. 1887. Courtesy of IU Archives (P0020559).

Owen Hall, c. 1889. Photograph by A. J. Summers, Bloomington, Indiana. Courtesy of IU Archives (P0022262).

1891

The program Physical Training for Men traces its beginnings to 1891 and the first men's gymnasium, which was built behind Owen Hall. James Lilly Zink becomes Director of the Men's Gymnasium when it is opened in 1892.

First Men's Gymnasium behind Owen Hall, June 27, 1918. This image shows the first gymnasium that was built, in 1892. After the first Assembly Hall was built in 1896, this building was used as a carpenter shop. This building was located four feet west and seventy-one feet north of Owen Hall. Photograph by Henry Thew Stephenson. Courtesy of IU Archives (P0022843).

1896

The Women's Gymnasium moves to Mitchell Hall. A second men's gymnasium is constructed east of Owen Hall. The gymnasium is renamed Assembly Hall in 1917 and razed in 1938.

1897

The first elective Physical Education Program is initiated and is variously known as class work, practice, and service.

Mitchell Hall (also known as Maxwell Hall), August 22, 1940. Photograph by IU Photographic Services. Courtesy of IU Archives (P0033665).

Assembly Hall, c. 1938. Photograph by IU Photographic Services. Courtesy of IU Archives (P0030588).

1917

A new men's gymnasium is completed, followed by the construction of an attached field house, completed in 1928 and later renamed the Wildermuth Intramural Center. The HPER addition to this building complex is completed in 1960.

Men's Gymnasium, c. 1920. The Men's Gym was completed in 1917. The Ora L. Wildermuth Fieldhouse and School of HPER buildings were not added to this structure until later. Courtesy of IU Archives (P0026802).

1920

Professor George Schlafer develops and teaches the first recreation course, The Nature and Practice of Play. By the 1930s, Professor Schlafer is teaching, promoting, and directing recreation courses throughout Indiana.

1922

The Physical Education for Women and Hygiene and Physical Education for Men and Hygiene programs are both established in the College of Arts and Sciences, as evolved from the earlier programs of physical training for women and men.

1925

The first Master of Arts degree in Education/Physical Education from the College of Arts and Sciences is conferred upon Curtis Kirklin. His thesis is titled "The Administration of Athletic Funds in Indiana High Schools."

1926

Martha Carr is awarded the first Bachelor of Science degree in Women's Physical Education under the auspices of the School of Education.

1931

The Department of Physical Welfare Training is established in the School of Education with emphases in health, hygiene, physical education, coaching, recreation, safety, and public health nursing. By 1933, W. W. Patty is listed in the Indiana University catalog as the director of and a professor in this department.

1932

The first Doctor of Education in physical education is awarded to John Harmon. The title of his dissertation is "Methods of Procedure in the City Comprehensive School Health and Physical Education Survey."

1938

Faculty members in the areas of health, physical education, and recreation are polled by W. W. Patty. They overwhelmingly approve the concept of the School of Health, Physical Education, and Recreation. This poll is followed in 1940 with an official vote for a separate school. World War II precludes further movement on the idea until the mid-1940s.

1942

World War II sparks the development of a massive physical fitness program on campus.

1945

At the September meeting, the Board of Trustees of Indiana University authorizes the formation of the School of Health, Physical Education, and Recreation.

July 1, 1946

The Indiana University School of Health, Physical Education, and Recreation is established and becomes fully operational. W. W. Patty assumes leadership as dean. Administrative offices are housed in Mottier Hall.

Mottier House, April 13, 1942. The first home for the School of HPER Administrative Offices in 1946. In this image, Alpha Hall is the building at the extreme right, the building just visible on the left is the old IU health center, and the limestone building in the background is the west side of Goodbody Hall. Photograph by IU Photographic Services. Courtesy of IU Archives (P0037589).

2

The Creation and Growth of HPER

THE NATION WAS BEGINNING A PERIOD OF RELATIVE prosperity when the School of HPER was beginning its life as an autonomous unit in 1946. The postwar era saw the return of a level of normalcy to the Bloomington campus, and enrollments began to increase dramatically. The benefits that veterans received from the Servicemen's Readjustment Act, the so-called GI Bill of Rights (1944), contributed much to this growth. Indiana University was the first in the country to enroll veterans supported by the GI Bill. Enrolled veterans for the spring semester of 1946 numbered 2,895 and the projection for the fall semester was for more than four thousand.

As the nation moved away from a war economy and toward a consumer culture, higher education became a commodity within reach of millions of Americans. Ordinary citizens and veterans helped the campus grow from 5,560 students in 1940 to 10,713 in 1950, and to over 30,000 by 1970. While total enrollments on the Bloomington campus were soaring, so too were the enrolled majors in the School of HPER. The school recorded 222 undergraduate and 79 graduate majors during the spring semester of 1947, and it would experience steady growth in student majors throughout its first twenty-five years. By the fall semester of 1970 the number of majors was 728 undergraduate and 291 graduate.

With the nation prospering on all fronts, the president and trustees of Indiana University felt that service to the state, nation, and professions was as important as meeting the needs of the students and campus. Members of the faculty were highly involved in the provision of outreach activities. Under the direction of Professor Karl Bookwalter, the Bureau of Service and Research supported consultants and the faculty responded to requests for assistance in areas such as facilities, tests and measurements, research, higher education, training and

(facing) Wells welcoming World War II veterans who would be living in the board room/conference room during the housing shortage, October 1946. Photograph by IU Photographic Services. Courtesy of IU Archives (P0023856).

Bradford Woods: A Crown Jewel

In 1938, John Bradford deeded nine hundred acres of Bradford Woods to Indiana University. Bradford Woods was the first gift received by Herman B Wells after his inauguration as President of Indiana University. Upon Bradford's death, the university received another fourteen hundred acres. In 1992, Wells explained the acquisition of Bradford Woods in this way:

> The secretary of Hugh Landon, President of the Riley Association, was a cousin of John Bradford and his brother. She visited the brothers and their old maid sister who were thinking about what to do with a considerable portion of the land. They had been in the molding sand business. Included was some bottom land, farm land, which they sold. The question was what should they do with a large tract of wooded hills? How could it be made effective and useful? The Riley Association had always been a public/private cooperative thing. I was on the Riley board and Jim Carr was its president at that time. We got the idea that this property could be used as a crippled children's camp. That was the first idea. We had to convince the professional staff at Riley Hospital that they could work with kids outside the hospital. This was no easy task. They had a good many reasons to believe you couldn't take care of kids outside the hospital. But, we got that job done. We went to see John Bradford on a number of occasions and suggested that he might want to give that great tract of land for outdoor recreation, particularly for crippled children. That was the first thrust of it. The idea appealed to the Bradfords so they gave us all that land plus a considerable endowment. We then went to work developing camps. Riley came, the Girl Scouts, and many others. Riley camp became the spring thing for school children of the state who needed an outdoor experience.

Perhaps no other entity of the school was addressed so frequently at the IU Board of Trustees Meeting as Bradford Woods, especially in the school's first

Bradford Woods Manor House, August 24, 1953. Photograph by IU Photographic Services. Courtesy of IU Archives (P0026756).

twenty-five years of operation. During this time, the university had agreements with various groups that leased property on, and enjoyed use of, Bradford Woods. Among them were the James Whitcomb Riley Memorial Association, the Central Indiana Council of the Boy Scouts of America, the Campfire Girls, the American Camping Association (ACA), and the Tulip Trace Girl Scout Council. Construction of Camp Riley had begun by 1952. Plans submitted by the Central Indiana Council of the Boy Scouts of America detailed improvements in the Boy Scout area of the Bradford Estate, which consisted of an entrance gate, a storage building, a kitchen and dining unit, a caretaker's cabin, and a latrine. These improvements started in the spring of 1953 at no expense to the university.

In 1952–1953, the first course was taught at Bradford Woods, by Reynold Carlson. The next year, Bradford Woods became fully operational under Resident Director Robert Tully. The ACA conducted its annual conference at Bradford Woods that same year, the first such event at this site, and Bradford Woods completed its first year of operation as a recreational training laboratory. The ACA returned in November 1953 to inaugurate the use of Bradford Lodge as a meeting center and was followed throughout the year by a number of other organizations. Improvements at Bradford Woods included a remodeling of the Bradford House and the Resident Director's house, preliminary construction of access roads, the provision of twenty trailers for graduate student housing, the provision of a water system, and the partial installation of a washhouse unit. The Board of Governors of the James Whitcomb Riley Memorial Association considered the expenditure of $73,250 from the Bradford Gift Fund for the benefit of the Bradford Woods Recreation Center. This was but one example of the ongoing relationship between the Riley Memorial Association and IU on the development, maintenance, and utilization of Bradford Woods.

A visit to the Bradford Woods property was on the program for the meeting of the IU Board of Trustees in October 1953. An informational statement covering the operation was given to each trustee. Funding, expenditures, and physical plant improvements were explained in detail. The trustees were informed that considerable importance was attached to a suitable name for the property inasmuch as indications pointed to the likelihood of this area as a nationally recognized top school in practical recreation instruction. The board adopted the name Bradford Woods, which was endorsed by the Riley Memorial Association.

By 1954–1955, a lodge and infirmary together with twenty-one small cabins for Camp Riley were erected, and the following year additional facilities were built, including twenty-four-person winterized cabins, a crafts building, and a swimming pool. Further, the Board of Trustees leased a tract of land to the ACA for the purposes of erecting and operating its National Headquarters.

Bradford Woods operated without a deficit for the first time in 1959–1960. A total of 41 conference groups involving 1,148 persons used the Bradford Manor House that year. Camp Riley hosted 19 different camping groups, totaling 2,049 campers. The next year, $280,000 was given by the Riley Memorial Association in support of a 110-acre lake that was completed in the fall of 1962.

In 1971–1972, a new master plan for Bradford Woods was in development with funding from the university research committee and the Riley Memorial Association. Bradford Woods was recognized as an important learning environment for the state of Indiana, as well as a national model. Also, in the same year, approval was given to a combined Camp Fire Girls–Girl Scouts proposal to construct a swimming pool on property leased to them under a fifty-year-term lease.

In 1974–1975 the first phase of Camp Riley Outdoor Center was completed at a cost of approximately $500,000. Improvements to the facilities included the building of six accessible residential lodges, waterfront expansion, and the installation of more than one mile of accessible nature trails. All renovations were approved by the Board of Trustees. Trustee Joseph M. Black enthusiastically endorsed IU President John Ryan's request that Robert Baxter be commended for the development of Camp Riley, which held the promise of becoming the finest such camp in the entire country. Further construction projects in 1975–1976 included the completion of the Camp Riley Outdoor Center dining hall, craft lodge, nature lodge, and heated swimming pool, followed the next year with a new activities center and a wheelchair-accessible summer camp garden. A highlight of this period was an address from Indiana Governor Otis Bowen at the Second Outdoor Education Assembly, held in October 1978. The camp amphitheater was completed in 1979, and the new infirmary was dedicated on July 10 of that year.

The 1980s ushered in new programs when Bradford Woods received a grant from the Indiana Department of Public Instruction for the purpose of developing training and outdoor education programs for special education teachers and their students. Additional funds would come from the Lilly Endowment through the Riley Memorial Association for improvements to Camp Riley. By the summer of 1982, the four bathing beaches on the 110-acre lake were ready and opened for use.

During the 1982–1983 academic year, Bradford Woods received national accreditation by the ACA with 98-percent scores in site approval and overall program. A new Adventure Challenge course was constructed, followed by the completion of the new Bradford Woods Administration Building the next year. By the 1984–1985 academic year, Bradford Woods had achieved an attendance record of over twenty thousand people. And it had achieved a balanced budget for the fifth year in a row, with income exceeding one million dollars for the first time in its history. During the year, the specialized Fitness Trail was dedicated, thus further expanding its outstanding facilities.

The University entered a fifty-year lease in 1985 with the ACA for a two-and-three-quarter-acre tract of land for its national offices. This use of the land was seen as beneficial to the school's academic mission in the field of recreation.

By the 1993–1994 academic year, renovation and restoration of the Bradford Woods Manor House was needed and a challenge grant from the Lilly Endowment supported the initiation of the project. During the school's fiftieth anniversary celebration in 1996–1997, a rededication of the Bradford Manor House was held. By then, the Manor House was on the National Register of Historic Places, thus bringing further recognition to Bradford Woods as an exemplary facility. Throughout the history of the school, Bradford Woods has excelled as a model site for outdoor recreation and outdoor education programs.

conferences, reference materials, and consultation. In addition, many official workshops, seminars, and institutes were sponsored by the school and its departments. These events exemplified the school's ongoing commitment to service and outreach. The following were just some of the official workshops/institutes held by the school during its first twenty-five years of operation.

In the Department of Health and Safety, the Annual School and Community Health Workshop was an ongoing activity, the fourth workshop being held in 1946–1947. These workshops continued for twenty-three years, ending in 1965–1966. The department also offered many other institutes and workshops involving health-related topics, such as an Institute on Family Life Education, a Child Development and Family Life Education Workshop, and the Workshop on Problems of Alcoholism and Alcohol Education. It was common for these workshops to be cosponsored by such organizations and agencies in the state as the Indiana State Board of Health and the Indiana Department of Mental Health, among others. The department continued offering its premier workshops and institutes over the years and was a leader in the state in addressing critical health problems.

The departments of Physical Education for Men and Physical Education for Women sponsored many events related to fitness and sport. The first Aquatic Leadership Workshop and the Conference for National Cooperation in Aquatics were first held in

(facing) Karl Bookwalter at the Audio Visual Picnic, June 1947. Photograph by IU Photographic Services. Courtesy of IU Archives (P0048351).

the 1960s. Also, a joint Symposium on Integrated Development was held in cooperation with Purdue University, the University of Wisconsin, and the Indiana State Board of Health. Other events included the Fourth National Institute of Girls' Sports, sponsored by the Women's Board of the Olympic Development Committee and the Division of Girl's and Women's Sports of the American Alliance for Health, Physical Education, and Recreation (AAHPER; later named the American Alliance for Health, Physical Education, Recreation, and Dance [AAHPERD]), and an Institute on Exercise and Conditioning Activities with a focus on the fitness of children and adults, cosponsored with the National YMCA.

The Department of Recreation became nationally recognized for the Great Lakes Park Training Institute, which was initiated in 1946–1947 by Garrett Eppley. Attendees came from throughout the United States and Canada. This institute continued annually as one of the most successful and enduring service activities of the department. Other departmental activities included a Park Lecturer Series established in the 1960s, which provided lectures on park and natural resource management. The Department of Recreation likewise provided early leadership in the area of therapeutic recreation. A well-attended Therapeutic Recreation Institute was held over three days in 1961–1962 and was made possible by a grant from the Indiana Department of Mental Health.

THE 1960S SHEPHERDED in the era of the Great Society and increased American involvement in the Vietnam War; both were to have an immense impact on universities and colleges around the country. It is difficult to overestimate the impact of this decade on American life. The 1960s were hailed as transformational, liberal, and forward thinking; they were also times of deep division. Not only was there a growing antiwar sentiment, but the Baby Boomers also were beginning to come of age. By

the mid-1960s, a new generation of college students was emerging, asking that their voices be heard and setting the stage for campus unrest.

Along with increasing prosperity had come noticeable economic disparities. Social inequalities due to race, age, and gender were entering the American consciousness. President Lyndon B. Johnson, following on the initiatives of the assassinated President John F. Kennedy, infused a government response to these inequalities with the big ideas and programs of his Great Society. Great Society programs came at the time when the post–World War II boom was beginning to fade and the country was becoming increasingly aware of new social needs.

The domestic agenda for the Great Society included expanded federal support for college students in the form of low-interest loans and scholarships. It is not an inconsequential fact that student enrollment on the Bloomington campus more than doubled between 1960 and 1970. Further, there were increased subsidies for libraries, classrooms, the development of community colleges and technical institutes, and new graduate centers, which all served to further advance postsecondary education.

During the 1960s, the School of HPER experienced significant change, signaled by the opening of a new HPER academic building. Original faculty members were retiring and new faculty were being appointed. Changes in leadership positions provided the impetus for new directions, beginning with the appointment of Dean Arthur S. Daniels in 1957 and the retirement of Mark Wakefield as Chair of the Department of Physical Education for Men in 1961. Dean Daniels' untimely death, on June 18, 1966, dealt the school a severe blow. At the time of Daniels' death, John Endwright had just begun his service as Chair of the Department of Physical Education for Men but was quickly appointed Acting Dean, becoming Dean in 1967. George Cousins assumed the position of Chair of the Department of Physical Education for Men.

(counterclockwise from top left)
HPER construction, October 1, 1959. Photograph by IU Photographic Services and William Stucker. Courtesy of IU Archives (P0026718).

HPER construction, November 30, 1959. Photograph by IU Photographic Services and Anderson. Courtesy of IU Archives (P0042364).

Royer Pool construction, December 6, 1960. Photograph by IU Photographic Services and Charles Dawson. Courtesy of IU Archives (P0026796).

HPER building, April 12, 1962. Photograph by IU Photographic Services and Ralph "Porky" Veal. Courtesy of IU Archives (P0042368).

(facing) Modern Dance Studio, August 10, 1961. Photograph by IU Photographic Services and Jim Newbury. Courtesy of IU Archives (P0037013).

By 1968, the administrative structure of the school had been reorganized with the appointment of John Cooper as Associate Dean of the Graduate Division and James Belisle as Assistant Dean of the Undergraduate Program. This new structure reflected the changing needs of the school, especially in the area of undergraduate and graduate education.

Wesley Dane, the first Chair of the Department of Health and Safety, was succeeded by Keogh Rash in 1952, who held both a Doctorate in Health and Safety and a Master's in Public Health. His professional qualifications enabled the widening of the agenda of the Department of Health and Safety Education, forging the way for a new Master of Public Health program.

In the Department of Physical Education for Women, Chair Edna Munro was succeeded by Naomi Leyhe in 1958, who was followed by Anita Aldrich in 1964. Aldrich quickly made her mark on the program and would make a significant contribution to the field of physical education. She served on the President's Council on Physical Fitness and the Advisory Committee of the Educational Policies Commission. Her involvement in curriculum development was considerable, enabled by Great Society legislation and funding through the Elementary and Secondary Education Act of 1965. Her pioneering efforts benefited multiple areas, including the creation of physical education curricula for children with cognitive impairments, and had a major impact on the participation of women in intercollegiate sports. Her awareness of opportunities and needs outside the immediate operation of the department clearly set the tone for the ensuing era.

Garrett Eppley retired as the second Chair of the Department of Recreation in 1962. Rey Carlson assumed the Chair, followed in 1966 by Ted Deppe. Throughout this period, the field was rapidly expanding to include specializations in outdoor recreation/outdoor education, recreation and park administration, resource management, campus recreation, college union management, and therapeutic recreation.

Along with the opening in 1961 of the new HPER building came a burst of fresh energy among the faculty and administration. Under the new leadership in the school, innovative initiatives were being developed. In keeping with President Wells' philosophy of hiring the best and leaving them to do the job, the school was well positioned to meet the opportunities and challenges that accompanied the Great Society.

It is noteworthy that by the mid-1960s, two departments had changed their titles to reflect their expanding horizons. The Department of Recreation became the Department of Recreation and Park Administration, and the Department of Health and Safety became the Department of Health and Safety Education.

As growing social unrest ushered in the 1970s, the school marked its first twenty-five years, observing its Silver Anni-

Danny Danielson, School of HPER administrators, and the president of the IU Board of Trustees confer on policy. From left to right: Dr. James Belisle, Assistant Dean for Undergraduate Development; Dr. John M. Cooper, Associate Dean and Chair of Graduate Division; Donald C. Danielson, President of Board of Trustees; Dean John R. Endwright. Photograph by IU News Bureau. Courtesy of IU Archives (P0049682).

(facing) HPER classroom, August 10, 1961. Photograph by IU Photographic Services. Courtesy of IU Archives (P0042359).

versary on December 17 and 18, 1971. The celebration was held in conjunction with the annual gathering of the HPER alumni, thus providing the occasion to draw together friends, as well as students, faculty, and staff, of the school. It was a time to reflect on a quarter century of growth and accomplishments. "Many memories are stirred by a Silver Anniversary," wrote Dean Endwright in the anniversary program.

It has been my privilege to have served the School since its birth, the first year as a teaching assistant, thereafter as a member of the faculty. I recall my many conferences with our first Dean, the beloved Dr. W. W. Patty. Just as vividly, but perhaps less fondly, I remember our move from Mottier House to Alpha Hall where we faced the flooded basement classrooms, graduate study cubicles, and research labs. The retirement of Dean Patty marked the end of a flourishing era in which we managed to overcome many obstacles.

Next, the faculty and administration were fortunate in acquiring the services of Dr. Arthur S. Daniels as our second Dean. Again, I have many memories of our numerous chats and conferences as we planned the development of our School. . . .

Fortunately my close relationship with and an understanding of the philosophies and goals of both of these fine gentlemen permitted us to bring to fruition some of the plans and programs they initiated. In tribute to these twenty-five years as well as in the interest of the future, faculty, students and alumni must dedicate their continued support as we strive to keep our place among the strong schools in the United States.

1946–1947

The School of HPER is officially opened on July 1, 1946, with its administrative offices in Mottier House.

Administrative positions for and the departmental structure of the School of Health, Physical Education, and Recreation are as follows:

Clara L. Hester, Director of the Normal College of the American Gymnastic Union

Mark Wakefield, Chair, Department of Physical Education for Men

C. Wesley Dane, Acting Chair, Department of Health and Safety

Karl Bookwalter, Director, Bureau of Service and Research

Edna Munro, Chair, Department of Physical Education for Women

George Schlafer, Chair, Department of Recreation

Alvin McMillin, Director, Intercollegiate Athletics

W. W. Patty, Director, Athletic Professional Training

Intercollegiate Athletics are administered by the Director of Athletics under the supervision of the Indiana University Athletic Faculty Committee and the President in accordance with the Western Athletic Conference regulations. Members of the Athletic Department also hold faculty appointments in the school.

During the school's first academic year, faculty members develop fifteen professional curricula in health and safety, physical education, and recreation. The Board of Trustees authorizes the school to grant the degree of Bachelor of Science in Public Health effective October 1, 1946, which represents the first degree of its kind in Indiana.

The campus recreation program is housed in the Department of Recreation. Garrett Eppley, Edna Munro, and Mark Wakefield organize a Campus Recreation Committee.

1948–1949

The HPER Alumni Newsletter is first published in December 1948.

The literary collection of alumnus Lebert H. Weir is donated to IU with the understanding that the Recreation Department would establish the L. H. Weir Library. Weir, a leader in the park and recreation field for almost forty years, authored many books and publications used in the field.

1950–1951

The school moves from Mottier House to Alpha Hall, which previously had been a women's dormitory, as well as a home for the School of Education.

Alpha Hall, probably 1961. Courtesy of IU Archives (P0026743).

1951–1952

The first Summer Alumni Conference is held on July 17, 1952, with two hundred alumni present. Intramural sports has become a highly successful program of seventeen different sport schedules with a total of 3,943 different men taking part during the year. The corresponding Women's Recreation Association conducts events in basketball, volleyball, swimming, golf, tennis, softball, hockey, bowling, badminton, and table tennis, with close to one thousand individuals participating.

1953–1954

Indiana University administration approves a new building for the School of HPER. The location is to be in the area of what was then called the Men's Gymnasium and Fieldhouse.

A new golf course is under construction. It will be sufficiently completed for an intercollegiate competition in the spring of 1957 and becomes fully operational that fall.

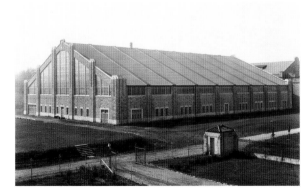

Wildermuth Fieldhouse, 1929. Photograph by Charles Gilbert Shaw. Courtesy of IU Archives (P0026774) and Mathers Museum of World Cultures, IU (1973-11-0013).

1954–1955

Dean W. W. Patty serves as Acting Director of Athletics until Frank E. Allen assumes the duties as Director of Athletics effective June 15, 1955.

1955–1956

Unchanged in ten years are the eight units that constitute the school:

Athletic Professional Training

Health and Safety Department

Normal College of the American Gymnastic Union

Department of Physical Education for Men

Department of Physical Education for Women

Recreation Department

Bureau of Service and Research

Intercollegiate Athletics

1956–1957

Arthur Simpson Daniels becomes the second Dean of the School of HPER on July 1, 1957.

The school offers 442 class sections in 202 different courses for a total enrollment of 11,251 students. In addition, there are 134 graduate students enrolled in individual research, field experiences, and theses. Putting HPER enrollment into perspective, university enrollment on the Bloomington campus for the spring semester was reported by the registrar to be 11,318 students.

1957–1958

In October 1957, construction begins on the new HPER building, which was then referred to as the Gymnasium Annex.

The First Annual Senior Send-Off Banquet is held.

1959–1960

The Woodlawn Tennis Courts are completed.

1960–1961

The Undergraduate Curriculum Study Committee revises the undergraduate curriculum requirements in line with new standards set forth by the State Department of Public Instruction.

The school moves from Alpha Hall to the new HPER building during Christmas recess 1960.

1961–1962

The first HPER High School Recruitment Day is held in October 1961.

HPER construction, May 29, 1959. Photograph by IU Photographic Services and Ralph "Porky" Veal. Courtesy of IU Archives (P0042366).

Entrance to HPER, Fall 1980. Photograph by IU News Bureau. Courtesy of IU Archives (P0042444).

On December 7–9, 1961, the HPER building is dedicated in a three-day gala affair, with an elaborate banquet and special presentations on "Research on the Aging Process" by David Dill (Research Scholar, Department of Anatomy and Physiology), "The Stress Concept in Conditioning Athletes" by "Doc" Counsilman, and "Movement Education: The Subject Matter of Physical Education" by Evelyn Davies. The annual Big Ten Meetings are held in conjunction with the dedication. Dean Emeritus W. W. Patty attends the ceremony, the only time he will return to campus following his retirement.

1961–1962

The Robert Royer Pool is dedicated on March 3, 1962, in memory of the IU swimming coach. The dedication is held in conjunction with the Big Ten Indoor 1962 Swimming Championships with President Wells presiding.

1964–1965
The IU Board of Trustees approves a change in name for the Department of Recreation to the Department of Recreation and Park Administration, effective July 1, 1964.

1965–1966
The US Commissioner of Education awards a grant to Anita Aldrich to support research directed toward the identification and evaluation of a conceptual framework for the physical education curriculum for K–16 (kindergarten through bachelor's degree).

The Board of Trustees approves a change in name for the Department of Health and Safety to the Department of Health and Safety Education, as well as the establishment of the Center for Safety and Traffic Education.

The University Outdoor Pool officially opens on Founder's Day, May 4, 1966.

1966–1967
In November 1966, President Stahr appoints a committee to study the proposed Center for Research in Outdoor Recreation. In April 1967, the committee submits its report to President Stahr. The Program for Research in Outdoor Recreation is approved by the Administrative Council of the university.

An exercise physiology laboratory fully equipped for faculty and student research becomes operational. Loren Myhre is appointed its director.

1967–1968
The PhD in human performance for physical education is approved by the Graduate Curriculum Council of the University Graduate School.

The Graduate Record Exam is required for all incoming graduate students beginning in September 1967.

1967–1968
The Modern Dance Performing Group presents concerts for the Indiana University Convocation Series, Normal College, and Culver Military Academy. Jacqueline Clifford, Program Director, is also choreographer for the IU Summer Opera production, Boito's *Mefistofele*.

Modern Dance, March 18, 1961. Photograph by IU Photographic Services. Courtesy of IU Archives (P0037031).

1968–1969
The Board of Trustees approves the Master of Public Health (MPH) degree.

1969–1970
The Board of Trustees approve naming the basketball playing floor in the new Assembly Hall the Branch McCracken Memorial Basketball Floor.

1970–1971
The School of Health, Physical Education, and Recreation celebrates its Silver Anniversary.

3

Years of Flourishing

DURING THE 1970S, SEVENTY MILLION BABY BOOMERS brought a free-spirited and somewhat revolutionary way of thinking to college campuses across the nation. While America continued to enjoy relative prosperity, change was on the horizon. The country's international stature had begun to decline politically, culturally, and economically. Taxes and cost of living increased, oil prices rose, foreign competition emerged, and the US dollar dropped in world markets, all of which began to test the future of American prosperity.

Along with the shifting character of American life, the 1970s were distinctly changing times in the school. Early in the decade, Dean Endwright continued to move the school along the path laid out by the initiatives that Deans Patty and Daniels had put into action. By the 1973–1974 academic year, the absorption of the Normal College by IUPUI was completed, and its name had been changed to the School of Physical Education. At the end of June 1975, Dean Endwright retired as dean and returned to full-time teaching. Professor Anita Aldrich was appointed as Acting Dean for 1975–1976. On July 1, 1976, Tony A. Mobley was appointed as the fifth dean of the School of HPER. Under his transformative leadership across twenty-six years, the school would grow to become the fourth-largest academic unit on the Bloomington campus. Mobley's unique ability to embrace all segments of the academic and professional communities was instrumental to the school's earning a national and international reputation as a leader in its field. Dean Mobley's daily administrative style reflected the philosophy that all people were important to the success of the school. His genuine and humble nature made him special to all the people who worked with him.

(facing) Tony Mobley, 1961. Photograph from the June 1, 2002, program honoring Mobley. Courtesy of IU School of Public Health–Bloomington.

Ushering in the Next Twenty-Five Years: From Dean Endwright's Annual Report to President Ryan, August 1972

Organizational Structure of the School

The organizational structure chart for the school consisted of Dean, Associate Dean for Graduate Faculty and Graduate Council, Assistant Dean for Faculty and Undergraduate Council, and six chairs for the following units: (a) Graduate Division, (b) Athletic Professional Training, (c) Department of Health and Safety Education, (d) Department of Physical Education for Women, (e) Department of Physical Education for Men, and (f) Department of Recreation and Park Administration.

Undergraduate Programs

Each department within the school had revised its undergraduate programs. The undergraduate student could specialize in one of four areas in recreation and park administration. In the Departments of Physical Education the undergraduate student could select specialization in such areas as adapted physical education, elementary physical education, dance in education, coaching, or general physical education. The major emphasis in health and safety education was the development of health and safety educators. Also, Indiana University was one of the first institutions to offer a specialization in athletic training. Many young men and women were now graduating from the undergraduate program as professional trainers.

Graduate Programs

During 1970–1972 the graduate faculty had revised their graduate programs to provide the student an opportunity to major in one of many areas of specialization, the basic philosophy being that the graduate degree should be tailored to meet the needs of the individual student. In addition to the master's degree, the school offered the director's degree (60 hours of graduate credit) for the professional preparation of supervisors, administrators, and master teachers in specific areas of concern. The doctoral degree permitted a higher level of specialization, and Indiana University had produced a legacy of placing many of the leading administrators, college and university teachers, and researchers at many institutions throughout the nation. The school had gained approval to offer the Master of Public Health degree. This degree program was expected to grow, based on the great need for this type of professional.

Within the previous five years the school in conjunction with the Graduate School had developed a PhD degree in Human Performance. Graduates with this degree were qualified to work as exercise physiologists, biomechanists, and motor learning experts.

Services to the Indiana University Student

The School made a unique contribution to the Indiana University student body through its many programs, both for credit and noncredit. These programs also required a considerable amount of faculty time. For instance, during 1971–1972 the men's intramural program had 17,514 participants. This involved, for example, 410 teams in basketball and 248 teams in football, along with many other team and individual sports. In addition, the department sponsored fourteen sports clubs. The women's intramural sports program was also growing rapidly, as shown during 1971–1972 with approximately 2,450 participants. The women also sponsored eight intercollegiate competitive sports teams coached and supervised by IU faculty and associate instructors.

Charting New Directions

As Dean Mobley assumed leadership of the school, he began a process of organizational change and development that reflected new priorities. In 1975, the school consisted of four academic departments, along with the Division of Graduate Studies and the Division of Recreational Sports. Mobley presented a new organizational chart that proposed administrative changes in the Dean's office, which would include an Associate Dean for Graduate Studies (John Cooper), an Associate Dean for Administration and Undergraduate Studies (James Belisle), an Assistant Dean for Research and Development (David Gallahue), a Coordinator of Continuing Education (Clinton Strong), and a Coordinator of Facilities and Equipment (Bob Hicks).

Because the departments of Physical Education for Men and Physical Education for Women had been approved for a merger, effective July 1, 1977, under the school's reorganization there now were three academic departments: Health and Safety Education, Recreation and Park Administration, and Physical Education.

In his August 1977 report to the Board of Trustees, Dean Mobley noted that the school was at a critical juncture with the retirement of a large number of nationally recognized faculty members. In large measure, the future would be determined by the extent to which talented and productive new faculty could be recruited and hired. In response to these coming changes and to the rapidly changing times, Dean Mobley initiated the development of a Long Range Master Plan.

As Mobley emphasized in his annual report for the academic year 1977–1978, increasing enrollments and high demand for the elective courses, recreational sports, and professional preparation programs were serious concerns. In addition, faculty members were highly engaged in research and service that stretched the school's resources and manpower needs.

Under Dean Mobley's leadership, the school embraced many initiatives associated with fitness and sports, including the Olympic movement and the National Training Program for Fitness and Health.

Throughout the school's history, faculty, coaches, and HPER majors were keenly involved with the Olympic movement. Many of the athletic coaches were also prominent members of the school faculty. Notable achievements included numerous years of coaching Olympic teams by "Doc" Counsilman (swimming), Hobie Billingsley (diving), and Jerry Yeagley (soccer). Yeagley also served as a member of the US Olympic Committee (USOC) and the Olympic Selection Committee, while Hobie Billingsley served as a member of the Olympic Diving Committee. In 1977–1978, James Wilkerson served on the USOC. Professor Phil Henson served as a referee for the track and field events at the 1984 Summer Olympic Games in Los Angeles. These are just a few examples of the many Olympic involvements by school faculty and coaches. In 2000, James Skinner received the prestigious Sport Science Award in the area of biomedical sciences from the International Olympic Committee.

Alumni, too, brought recognition for involvement in the Olympic movement. For example, a 1998 *HPER Dimensions* feature story reported that Tom Crawford (PhD, 1989) had served as the Director of Coaching for the USOC. The spotlight of involvement in Olympic-related activities was ever present.

Professors Clint Strong and Scott Greer were deeply involved in the activities of the Education Committee of the USOC in the 1970s and 1980s. They organized special educational symposiums and Olympic Academies held at various sites throughout the United States as well as in Olympia, Greece. In 1978–1979, Strong and Greer together completed the preliminary work for the NOA-Session IV, which was held at Indiana University May 29–June 1, 1980.

In 1979, Clint Strong was asked by the USOC to be one of a group of six educators from the United States who would present papers at the Third International Session for Educationists

Hobie Billingsley, 1974. Photograph by the Athletic Department. Courtesy of IU Archives (P0028235).

James Counsilman, 1986. Photograph by the Athletic Department. Courtesy of IU Archives (P0022995).

Jerry Yeagley, 1979. Photograph by the Athletic Department. Courtesy of IU Archives (P0027295).

at Olympia, Greece. This session was held in conjunction with the Nineteenth Annual International Olympic Academy. Strong's topic was marketing the Olympic movement in the schools. Following the NOA-Session IV, Strong participated in a USOC Education Council planning session for National Olympic Academy V, June 8–13, 1981, held at the USOC Training Center in Colorado Springs.

Strong's involvement with the Olympic movement came at a time when international politics were played out in the Olympic arena. The United States used, as part of a package of political actions, a boycott of the 1980 Summer Olympics in Moscow as a means for protesting the Soviet invasion of Afghanistan. The United States threatened to boycott the Moscow Olympics if Soviet troops did not withdraw from Afghanistan within one month. A rejoinder by the Soviet Union indicated that they would boycott the 1984 Summer Olympics in Los Angeles in response to the boycott and what they saw as the anti-Soviet hysteria being stirred up in the United States. And in fact, both boycotts took place. In this context, it was important that the international and national Olympic organizations were pro-active in using the National Academies to promote the Olympic movement and its ideals, philosophies, and cultural value and the beauty of sport performance.

Beyond the faculty's involvement with the Olympics, the school was a leader in the fitness movement. In 1981–1982, the School of HPER became the administrative site for the Amateur Athletic Union (AAU) physical fitness testing and promotion program. Wynn Updyke served as Director. During his career at Indiana, Updyke secured over twenty-five separate contracts totaling over $15 million. Under his leadership, the AAU's President's Challenge Program touched the lives of over sixty million youths.

In 1984–1985, Dean Mobley and faculty from the Department of Physical Education were instrumental in establishing the National Institute for Fitness and Sport (NIFS) in Indianapolis. Leaders in this movement included Harold Morris, Department Chair; Wynn Updyke, Associate Dean of HPER; and Dean Mobley, who served as the Institute's first President. The school led the development of the Institute's $12 million complex. The NIFS, a not-for-profit organization housed on the IU campus in Indianapolis, was dedicated in a ceremony at its 18,000-square-foot facility on November 1, 1988. Leroy "Bud" Getchell, Professor of Physical Education, served as the Executive Director of the Institute. At the dedication, NIFS officials announced their long-term goals to help make Indianapolis the most physically fit community in the United States.

AS EARLY AS 1948–1949, the School of HPER was pioneering new curricula in athletic training. Dean Patty and Paul Harrell (Athletic Director and Director of the Athletic Professional Training Department) developed the first athletic training curriculum. Dwayne "Spike" Dixon served as the athletic trainer, and physician Charles Holland supervised the program. By the early 1980s, the growing interest in fitness and sports had spurred changes that moved IU's Athletic Training Program to

(overleaf) Promoting Physical Fitness, July 1989. Accompanying this image is an IU News Bureau release dated July 11, 1989, which reads, in full: "Both the Chrysler Fund-Amateur Athletic Union Physical Fitness Program and the President's Challenge National Youth Physical Fitness Program are administered through the Indiana University School of Health, Physical Education and Recreation. Each program is a nationwide outreach to American school children to promote physical fitness literacy. Director of the two programs is Wynn Updyke, Associate Dean for Academic Affairs at the school, left; Mike Willett, manager of the programs; and Laure Gentry, academic affairs coordinator at the school." Photograph by the IU News Bureau and Jerry Mitchell. Courtesy of IU Archives (P0042439).

John Schrader. Courtesy of IU School of Public Health–Bloomington.

Katie Grove. Courtesy of IU School of Public Health–Bloomington.

a level of sophistication that extended significantly beyond the scope of the program in 1949.

Dean Endwright reported that Indiana University was one of the first institutions to offer this specialization, and in 1977–1978, the undergraduate and graduate programs in Athletic Training were certified by the National Athletic Trainers'

Association (NATA). Because demand for the program was so great, limitations on enrollments had to be implemented.

Clinical Professors John Schrader and Katie Grove have been key players in the development and growth of the Athletic Training Program. "There was a time when people thought of athletic trainers merely as dispensers of tape and Ace bandages," noted John Schrader. "But today's athletic training student receives such extensive curricular and clinical experience that these stereotypes are gradually disappearing."

Indiana University's program remains one of only two athletic training programs in the nation that offer both undergraduate and graduate curricula approved by NATA. Alumni of the program have been successfully placed as teacher/trainers in high schools and colleges, athletic trainers in professional sports, and teachers in academic institutions.

Schrader and Grove have been recognized by NATA for their leadership. Schrader was inducted into the NATA Hall of Fame and Grove received the NATA Most Distinguished Athletic Trainer Award. In 2002–2003, Schrader was awarded the Golden Pinnacle Award by the Great Lakes Athletic Trainers' Association, and in 2013, he was the first recipient of the school's Distinguished Service Award for his pioneering leadership in the athletic training profession.

The Adult Fitness Program took the initiative in 1988 to develop an employee health and fitness program for the campus. Because positive health changes are more effective when incorporated into a fitness program, the focal point of the program was to promote a healthier lifestyle through exercise, physical activities, and nutrition. Important aspects of the program included the education and training of graduate students and research into the role of exercise in health promotion. Directors of the program were Jan Wallace and Chet Jastremski, MD. Alice Lindeman, PhD, RD, served as the nutrition coordinator for the program. Jan Wallace came to IU from San Diego State University, where she directed one of the oldest adult fitness programs in the country. Graduate students who were preparing for professional careers in corporate fitness, health promotion, and cardiac rehabilitation operated the program.

Envisioning the Future: The School's Strategic Plan

To plan is to anticipate the future by intelligent action now.
—HPER LONG-RANGE MASTER PLAN

In the 1970s and 1980s, in Indiana and throughout the world, waves of change were shaping a new economy in health, fitness, sport, and recreation. It was a cultural transformation that promised to be far reaching and growing in significance as the nation faced the onset of chronic diseases and new social problems associated with unhealthy behaviors. This new wellness movement marched to a different drummer, in step with the whir of disc drives and exercise cycles. It focused on quality-of-life goals for body, mind, and spirit. It addressed such issues as drugs and alcohol abuse, cancer, sexually transmitted diseases (STDs), fitness and nutrition, environmental quality, leisure and recreation, aging and the aged, and people with disabilities.

The wellness movement was advancing through research and education and reaching out to the masses with such technologies as telecommunications, networking, fiber optics, and computer graphics. It was high-tech, yet high-touch. Above all, it had limitless potential, for it drew its strength and energy from the greatest of all resources: the human mind.

The school's vision of the future at this juncture was guided by a continuing strategic planning process. During the school's fortieth anniversary year (1986–1987), the new long-range goals were shared with alumni, students, the administration, and faculty:

- To continue to attract the nation's finest students and faculty.
- To increase annual support for student assistance, library resources, and research.

- To establish an interdisciplinary institute in health and wellness, sport, and recreation.
- To provide resources for the expansion/renovation of facilities serving the school.

A foundation for accomplishing these goals was articulated in the school's strategic "quality-of-life" mission, which was "to facilitate healthful living, fitness, sport participation, and meaningful leisure/recreation through the provision of professional education, research, and leadership service to state, national, and international constituencies."

To accomplish this mission, the school capitalized on its legacy and reputation for outstanding leadership and superior performance. In a letter to IU President Thomas Ehrlich dated February 25, 1988, Dean Mobley noted that only IU and the University of Illinois, among schools with similar programs, could boast of having all disciplines and degrees ranked in the top six. Mobley also noted that only three educators had ever been elected to serve as presidents of the National Recreation and Park Association (NRPA) and that all three of these educators were on the School of HPER's faculty: James Peterson, Herbert Brantley, and Tony Mobley. Likewise, three additional members of the faculty had served as presidents of the American School Health Association: John Seffrin, Donald Ludwig, and Keogh Rash. Further, four faculty members had served as presidents of the American Alliance for Health, Physical Education, Recreation, and Dance (AAHPERD): Arthur Daniels, John Cooper, Harold Morris, and Anita Aldrich. In addition, a large number of faculty members provided similar leadership service at state, local, and university levels. Dean Mobley noted that 52 percent of all departments, divisions, or schools involving health, physical education, and recreation in the country were headed by graduates of the IU School of HPER.

John R. Seffrin

John R. Seffrin was appointed Professor and Chair of the Department of Health and Safety Education in 1979; in 1989 he took on the additional role of Director of the Center for Health and Safety Studies. During his tenure in the school, Seffrin was instrumental in leading the department forward in addressing problems pertaining to public health, particularly in the areas of tobacco use and cancer. He became Vice President of the American Lung Association of Indiana and was elected to the Board of Directors of the American Lung Association in 1979. He also was an elected delegate to the American Cancer Society. In 1985–1986, Seffrin served as Vice President of the American School Health Association and subsequently served as its president. In the early 1990s, Seffrin took a continuing leave of absence from IU to serve the American Cancer Society, first as Chair of the Board and later as CEO. A widely recognized leader in public health, Seffrin was named a Sagamore of the Wabash, received an Outstanding Alumnus Award from Ball State University, and was awarded honorary doctoral degrees from Indiana University, Purdue University, and Ball State University. John Seffrin's leadership and ongoing support greatly enhanced the reputation of the school and its advancement in the field of public health.

John Seffrin, July 5, 1984. Photograph by IU Photographic Services. Courtesy of IU Archives (P0053099).

Reporting to the Indiana University Board of Trustees on campus productivity, Chancellor Kenneth Gros Louis highlighted the productivity of the school. The Board's minutes summarize his presentation:

> In the School of Health, Physical Education and Recreation the teaching norm is 2 courses per semester. Peers, CIC schools, are similar, although Michigan and Illinois average less than four courses per year. Average course sections for Fall '89 were 3.9 and for Fall '92 were 3.7. Chancellor Gros Louis posed the question, "Why so high?" and said that a lot of courses taught in HPER are one-credit courses. Turning to research in the same period, . . . the number of awards increased from 10 to 22, the dollars increased from $905,000 to $2.8 million, and the indirect cost increased from $13,000 to $350,000. Further, Dean Tony Mobley of HPER writes, "While no other institution with similar programs has a policy of assigning more than two courses, we also teach more courses per faculty member, but according to most recent data, we generate more credit hours per faculty member than any other unit in the Big Ten."

During this period the school was clearly thriving, with a high level of productivity and new initiatives. Campus recreation was growing by leaps and bounds, and new centers and institutes were being started. Programs grew and faculty members were busier than ever.

Recreational Sports

The school has a long history of cultivating campus recreation and intramural sports as central to campus life. As early as 1951, Janet MacLean was hired to serve as both Instructor of Recreation and Campus Recreation Consultant, thus signaling IU's commitment to serving the recreational needs of its students. In 1967, a Campus Plan for Recreational Facilities was presented to the Board of Trustees that signaled a planned approach regarding the facilities and program needs of the campus. Planning recreation for the students attending Indiana University had always been carefully considered by the school in cooperation with the halls of residence, the architect's office, and the administration. Growth in the student population, however, had caused many changes in the design of recreation facilities. Consequently, a comprehensive master plan for recreation was needed to avoid costly errors. This plan signaled a coming era that eventuated in the creation of a separate Division of Recreational Sports in the school.

By the early 1970s, the intramural program for men and women had expanded considerably, with a minimum of ten thousand participants daily. The need for increased staff, funding, and facilities became more evident year by year. The impact of the growth in intramural sports spurred the development of an academic specialization for the training of intramural sports directors at the master's degree level in 1972.

The academic year of 1973–1974 was a pivotal one in the institutionalization of recreational sports under the management of the School of HPER. Richard F. Mull had been appointed as Director of Intramural Sports and Assistant Professor of Physical Education for Men. Both men's and women's intramural sports were unified under the Division of Recreational Sports. In the same year, the Board of Trustees approved a major plan for increasing recreational and intramural facilities on the Bloomington campus.

This was also the year that the Student Recreational Sports Committee was formed to provide greater student governance and to improve lines of communication between students and staff.

By 1975–1976, participation in recreational sports had grown to 28,500 students and others. The Division of Recreational Sports consisted of six programming areas: Women's Intramurals, Men's Intramurals, Co-Intramurals, Special Events, Sports Clubs, and Unstructured Activity. This was also the year that the division inaugurated the Spirit of Sport All-Nighter as a special fundraising event to benefit the Special Olympics. Participation in Recreational Sports continued to grow; by 1976–1977, participants numbered 34,877, a 22-percent increase over the previous year. With such sustained growth, the Campus Recreation Committee and the school endorsed a progressive dedicated fee to support operations and future facilities for Recreational Sports.

On May 4, 1979, Dean Mobley formally presented a Recreational Sports proposal to the Board of Trustees. The proposal included a dedicated student fee to fund the construction of the new facility. Hampered by university-wide budget concerns and declining undergraduate enrollment, the trustees took up discussion of the proposed student recreation center at their meeting in December 1979. Among the concerns were the proposed budget and the use of student dedicated fees for funding the project, with additional funds from the intercollegiate athletics program if a swimming pool that would satisfy intercollegiate competition requirements could be included. When the whole package was put together, the cost was estimated at somewhere in the neighborhood of $18,250,000. This meant that each student would pay around $35 per semester, which far exceeded the Student Association's recommendation of $20 per semester. There was additional concern that most facilities of this kind also included an academic component, while the current facility proposal did not. Further, it was known that the Indiana Commission for Higher Education would not approve planning money for nonacademic buildings. The high priority given to academic facilities on the Bloomington campus took precedence over development of a recreational sports facility. Considering these financial concerns, the Board's recommendation was to attempt to repackage the proposal to include academic programs before moving ahead with the project.

By the spring of 1980, all preliminary planning was completed for the new facility and the proposal was, once again, brought to the Board of Trustees at their April meeting. The revised proposal met both the recreational and research needs of the School of HPER and included a fifty-meter pool to serve the men's and women's intercollegiate athletic teams. The Board of Trustees was requested to make application to the Indiana Higher Education Commission for $200,000 in planning funds. At the meeting, Dean Mobley made note of the growth in physical activity throughout the entire nation in recent years. He also noted that IU had not developed any indoor facilities for recreational sports or physical activity since 1959. The present overcrowded and inadequate facilities had the capacity to serve only about 70 percent of the students.

Dean Mobley added that the proposal had been widely discussed and enjoyed strong support from a wide variety of campus groups, and the Board of Trustees unanimously approved the request. At the meeting of the trustees in November 1980, University President John Ryan reported that the proposed new recreational sports building was the last of twenty-nine projects that the Higher Education Commission had recommended to the General Assembly, which was indeed fortunate considering how many projects were left off the final list. Effective July 1, 1981, the Board of Trustees approved a public user fee for informal sports. The fee schedule included $50 per individual, $60 per family, and a $2 per day guest pass.

At their December 1989 meeting, the Board of Trustees passed a resolution acknowledging IU's national leadership in intramural sports, as well as intercollegiate swimming and diving, which offered further evidence of the need for a recreational sport and aquatic facility. The resolution appointed alumnus andIU Trustee, Frank E. McKinney, Jr., of Indianapolis, as National Chair for financial support for the new center. At last, the facility could be put out for bidding and contracting. The project as proposed called for the building of a structure of 141,194 assignable square feet to house recreational activities, an aquatic facility suitable for National Collegiate Athletic Association dual-meet competition, and instructional activities.

The completion of this building corrected many of the recreational sports space deficiencies on the Bloomington campus. Construction began in 1992 and, in the same year, Kathy Bayless was appointed Director of the Division of Recreational Sports. The much anticipated, $22 million, state-of-the-art Student Recreational Sports Center opened in the summer of 1995 and was officially dedicated in September. The Board of Trustees approved the following official names for the building's components: the James E. "Doc" Counsilman Aquatic Center, the Hobart S. "Hobie" Billingsley Diving Center, and the Frank E. McKinney, Jr., Hall.

In 1997, the Division of Recreational Sports reported a record year, with more than 1.5 million visits for self-directed participation in programs and activities offered by the division.

Other Programs, Institutes, and Centers

The Department of Health and Safety Education entered the 1970s with a distinguished history of involvement in safety education. The US Naval Safety School was established in 1972. The following year a Certificate program and Associate's degree in Hazard Technology were developed under the leadership of Bernard Loft. By the mid-1970s, two new undergraduate

Student Recreational Sports Center grand opening, September 15, 1995. From left to right: Myles Brand, Kenneth R. R. Gros Louis. Photograph by IU Photographic Services. Courtesy of IU Archives (P0042377).

At their meeting in April 1983, the trustees accepted the preliminary planning for the recreational sports facility. By this date, progress had been made toward identifying funding for the recreational sports facility as had been reported to President Ryan. Events unfolded slowly but steadily. At the May 1987 trustees meeting, Vice President Terry Clapacs reported on the ongoing study of a potential site for the building east of Jordan and north of Law Lane that was within a five-minute walk of about 70 percent of student housing. By the 1989–1990 academic year, detailed planning by the architects for the approximately $20-million new facility was nearly completed.

nonteaching options were developed, one of which was the Specialist in Occupational Safety. At the end of the 1970s, the Advisory Committee of the Hazard Control Program had approximately fifty short-course proposals approved for continuing education units by the School of Continuing Studies. These short courses enabled career and civilian military personnel to receive continuing education units toward Associate and Bachelor of Science degrees. The next year, the Hazard Control Program was transferred from the Division of General and Technical Studies to the Department of Health and Safety. This move enhanced the overall operation of the long-range goals in the area of occupational safety and hazard control.

The Hazard Control Program, funded through an Educational Services Contract with the US Navy, expanded in scope and magnitude. The 1979 contract (for $691,971) was the largest ever received and was the single-largest award of this nature on the Bloomington campus at the time. The provision of safety education and support services to the Naval Sea Systems Command (NAVSEA) Safety School constituted the main mission of the Hazard Control Program. The mission embraced services related to research, academic support, and demonstration projects delivered by a fifteen-member staff including two health and safety education faculty, nine adjunct faculty, numerous educational consultants, and graduate assistants.

The Certificate Program and Associate of Arts in Hazard Control Technology were subsequently modified to better reflect the philosophies of the school, as well as recent developments in the field of occupational safety and health. With the addition of these two programs, the Department of Health and Safety Education was positioned to develop a comprehensive vertical curriculum in public safety and health that was highly responsive to the job market. The available options for students included a one-year Certificate, a two-year Associate of Arts, a Bachelor of Science with a Concentration in Occupational Safety and Health, and a Master of Science in Health and Safety with Concentration in Safety Risk Management. Employment opportunities for graduates in these programs were very strong as Americans were demanding safe and healthful environments for work, home life, and leisure. The relationship between Indiana University and the US Navy was unique and mutually advantageous.

THE NATIONAL HEALTH EDUCATION HONORARY SOCIETY, Eta Sigma Gamma, was formally established when the articles of incorporation were filed with the State of Indiana on August 14, 1967, and the initiation of its first thirty members took place on the campus of Ball State University in Muncie, Indiana, on May 12, 1968. As with any new organization, Eta Sigma Gamma's major intent in its first years was to establish new chapters and recruit members. On March 22, 1974, fifty-six undergraduate and graduate majors in IU's Department of Health and Safety Education were initiated as charter members of the newly chartered Nu Chapter of Eta Sigma Gamma.

The purpose of Eta Sigma Gamma is to elevate the standards, ideals, competence, and ethics of professionally trained men and women in and for the health science discipline through teaching/education, service, and research. It maintains an official newsletter, *The Eta Sigma Gamman*, and a refereed professional journal, *The Health Educator: Journal of Eta Sigma Gamma*. It also maintains a *National Directory of College and University School and Public Health Educators*. A further contribution to the profession is the publication of the *Eta Sigma Gamma Monograph Series*.

Since its founding, Eta Sigma Gamma has grown to become the premier health honorary for health educators. By August 2012, the honorary had installed 127 chapters on university and college campuses. Eta Sigma Gamma has honored many HPER faculty and Nu Chapter members, including the following honorees:

Bill Yarber, August 27, 1993. Photograph by IU Photographic Services. Courtesy of IU Archives (P0053065).

- Keogh Rash was the recipient of the first annual Eta Gamma Honor Award in New York City at the Annual Meeting of the American School Health Association.
- Donald Ludwig received the Honor Award from Eta Sigma Gamma.
- Morgan Pigg received the National Distinguished Service Award from Eta Sigma Gamma.
- David Birch served as a faculty sponsor of the Nu Chapter when the chapter won the National Eta Sigma Gamma Teaching Award.
- James Crowe received the prestigious 2000 Eta Sigma Gamma Distinguished Service Award.
- The Department of Applied Health Science received national recognition with a 2002 Honor Award from Eta Sigma Gamma. This award is the highest honor bestowed upon an individual or institution in recognition of outstanding accomplishments in health education.

FOUNDED IN 1994, THE RURAL CENTER for AIDS/STD Prevention (RCAP) promotes HIV/STD prevention in rural America to reduce HIV/STD prevalence. At its founding, the center was a joint project between Indiana University and Purdue University, with William L. Yarber as Senior Director. The Center, sponsored by the US Congress, received funding from the Extension Service of the US Department of Agriculture and has continued throughout the history of the school to provide cutting-edge research and resources related to HIV/STD prevention.

In 2014, the RCAP had evolved into a joint project of Indiana University Bloomington, University of Colorado Denver, and the University of Kentucky. The Rural Center for AIDS/STD Prevention, based in the Department of Applied Health Science, was supported, in part, through a cooperative agreement with the Centers for Disease Control and Prevention (CDCP). In 2014, RCAP celebrated its twentieth anniversary.

A Rich Heritage and a Visionary Future:
Fiftieth Anniversary Celebration Program, January 20, 1996

Contemporary Distinctions

Indiana University's School of Health, Physical Education, and Recreation was widely recognized as one of the world's foremost institutions in the provision of higher education and research for the professions in kinesiology, applied health science, and recreation and park administration. The essence of HPER's dynamic academic community was threefold: our people, namely, the students, faculty, staff, and alumni who were serving with energy and wisdom; our challenge and timely mission of responding to the needs of a nation where body and intellect are healthy and fit; and our vision of providing nationally ranked academic programs in professional preparation and leading-edge research that make a difference in human values. Here are some of the highlights of HPER's distinctions at the time of its fiftieth anniversary:

HPER STUDENTS

- Almost 1,800 undergraduate and graduate declared majors in HPER.
- 12,500 students enrolled in HPER classes each year.
- Students chose from fifteen degree programs at the undergraduate and graduate levels.
- Students participated in 15 academic organizations and 250 school-directed internships annually.

HPER GRADUATES

- More than 340 students graduated from IU's School of HPER each year.
- HPER's more than thirteen thousand alumni represented fifty states and forty-one countries.

HPER FACULTY

- Of the school's sixty-three full-time faculty members, twenty-three had served as presidents of national organizations and eleven were winners of university teaching awards.

- HPER faculty members collectively authored sixty-one books and published an average of ninety-five articles a year.
- HPER faculty taught 1,305 class sections and 226 laboratory sections each year.
- Ninety percent of all courses for majors were taught by full-time faculty.
- HPER faculty were awarded more than $2,500,000 the previous year for support of research and scholarship.

HPER RESOURCES

- HPER supported twelve community service and research centers and institutes.
- The HPER Library resources included more than 17,300 books, 400 journal titles, and 38 online abstract services.
- The school encompassed twelve thousand square feet of laboratory space for research and teaching.
- Fifty-three public access computers were available for student use.

HPER OUTREACH

- Through adult fitness services, 250 individuals were enabled to live a healthier lifestyle each year.
- HPER provided training and certification for 650 people yearly in first aid and CPR.
- Each year twenty-six thousand students were served through Division of Recreational Sports programs and facilities.
- More than 530 children and youth with disabilities participated in summer camp at HPER's facilities annually.

As of this writing, William Yarber continues as Senior Director of RCAP. Yarber, Professor of Applied Health Science, Professor of Gender Studies, and Senior Research Fellow of the Kinsey Institute for Research in Sex, Gender, and Reproduction at IU, has written four school AIDS/STD curricula, including the nation's first school AIDS curriculum. His research focuses on examining HIV/STD risk behavior, particularly among youth and rural populations.

ON FEBRUARY 15, 1994, the Board of Trustees established the Eppley Institute for Parks and Public Lands in the Department of Recreation and Park Administration. James Ridenour, alumnus and former Director of the National Park Service, was appointed as Director. Ridenour had just completed his appointment as National Park Service Director and had previously served as Director of the Indiana Department of Natural Resources. The Institute was named in honor of Garrett G. Eppley, second Chair of the Department of Recreation. Eppley was an early pioneer in recreation and park education, as well as a well-known interpreter, trainer, and National Park Service recreation planner.

The mission of the Eppley Institute is to partner with recreation, park, and public land organizations to enhance access, choice, and quality of natural, cultural, and recreational experiences. The Eppley Institute continued throughout the history of the school to bring recognition and significant grant-funded projects to Indiana University.

HPER Turns Fifty

The academic year of 1995–1996 marked the school's Golden Anniversary. It was a time to reflect on and celebrate the school's accomplishments and contemplate new directions. At this juncture in the school's history, it was recognized that the HPER fields had logged a century of service dating back to the first courses in health, fitness, sport, and recreation that were taught at Indiana University in the 1890s. Events to celebrate the fiftieth anniversary included the dedication of the new recreational sports complex, alumni celebrations held at national conventions of HPER professional associations, commissioned art pieces that commemorated the various buildings that had housed HPER over the years, HPER Alumni Association–sponsored events, distinguished lectures, the rededication of the Bradford Manor House, and the development of an anniversary edition of *HPER Dimensions*.

During the anniversary year, a new Academic Endowment Campaign was in development and preparations for the future were in full swing. Facilities would need to be repaired, renovated, and upgraded. As the school continued to flourish, new academic appointments would be needed to fill the needs associated with the health, fitness, and wellness areas. Few could imagine that the twenty-first century would usher in new challenges and calls to action that would fundamentally change the school.

Highlights from the Era, 1971–1996

1971–1972
The Department of Physical Education for Women becomes a Charter Member of the Association for Intercollegiate Athletics for Women, the first governing body of intercollegiate athletics for women.

The first MPH degrees in the Department of Health and Safety Education are granted.

1972–1973
First Annual Campus Health Fair is held by the Department of Health and Safety Education.

1973–1974
Women's Intercollegiate Athletics moves to the IU Department of Athletics; Leanne Grotke is appointed Associate Director of Athletics.

1974–1975
The biomechanics and exercise physiology labs are upgraded and noted as among the best equipped in the nation.

1975-1976
The Wildermuth Fieldhouse renovation is completed.

The thirtieth year of the Great Lakes Park Training Institute is held under the leadership of Professors Dick Lawson and Don Martin. Over four hundred people register for the institute and more than fifty people present papers.

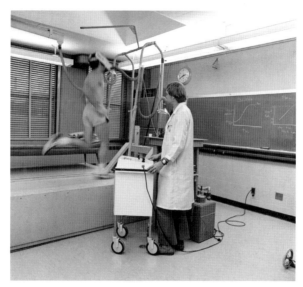

Classroom experiment, January 13, 1976. Photograph by IU Photographic Services and Tom Casella. Courtesy of IU Archives (P0026828).

1976–1977
Two new undergraduate nonteaching options are developed in the Department of Health and Safety: Public Health Education Specialist and Specialist in Occupational Safety.

1977–1978
The Department of Physical Education for Men and the Department of Physical Education for Women are merged into the Department of Physical Education on July 1, 1977; Anita Aldrich is appointed Chair.

Basketball in Wildermuth Fieldhouse, 1988. Photograph by IU News Bureau and Annalese Poorman. Courtesy of IU Archives (P0042445).

1978–1979
The Department of Recreation and Park Administration is granted accreditation of its professional preparation curriculum in four undergraduate emphases: (a) Public Parks and Recreation, (b) Outdoor Recreation and Education, (c) Therapeutic Recreation, and (d) Recreation Programming by the National Council on Accreditation for a five-year period beginning March 1979.

The HPER Library is established as an official branch of the IU Library System.

1979–1980
A Master of Science degree option in Recreational Sport Management in the Department of Recreation and Park Administration is approved by the school's Graduate Council.

1980–1981
A major grant from the US Public Health Service ($58,812) is awarded for *An Intervention Project to Deter Cigarette Smoking and Alcohol Abuse in Monroe County, Indiana Children and Adolescents*. Overall, school grants and contracts continue to improve with a total of $1,231,112 in externally acquired support.

Indiana University holds the distinction of being the only college or university in the state of Indiana offering the Master of Public Health degree, and as of now, it is the oldest and longest-accredited public health degree in the state of Indiana.

A major new program, Sports Science, is developed in the Department of Physical Education. Further, a new Master of Science degree option in Sports Medicine and Physical Fitness is developed with plans for implementation in 1981–1982.

1981–1982
In four separate national surveys, all the academic fields (health, physical education, recreation, and parks) in the School of HPER are ranked at or near the top, with only one other institution, the University of Illinois, also ranked in the top six for all fields.

The Department of Recreation and Park Administration implements the TV-distributed education course Health for Aging.

1982–1983
The Department of Health and Safety Education focuses its undergraduate program in two areas: preparation for careers in community-based health education and preparation for certification in school health education. The department's graduate program establishes a PhD in Health Behavior. Additionally, IU becomes the first university in the nation to offer a doctorate in Health and Safety Education.

1983–1984
The US Fitness Academy, under the auspices of the National Fitness Foundation and the President's Council on Physical Fitness and Sports, is located in Indianapolis. Several HPER faculty members are involved in its founding: Physical Education Chair David Clarke, Associate Dean Wynn Updyke, and Dean Tony Mobley.

1984–1985
The trustees approve a name change for the Department of Health and Safety Education to the Department of Applied Health Science. Further, the newly transferred programs, faculty, and students in the areas of Human Development and Family Studies and of Nutrition and Dietetics become fully operational.

1985–1986
The Department of Physical Education develops a new two-year master's program in Preventive and Rehabilitative Exercise; Janet Wallace is appointed Director.

1986–1987
The School of HPER celebrates its fortieth anniversary. The number of majors enrolled during the fall semester includes 574 undergraduate and 250 graduate students. A total of 241 degrees are conferred between July 1, 1986, and June 30, 1987. In 1986–1987, the school produces a total of 38,999 credit hours.

Alumnus Dick Enberg (MS, 1959; HSD, 1962; Doctor of Humane Letters, 2002) is the inaugural speaker for the School of HPER Distinguished Lecture Series.

Dick Enberg Distance Education Studio dedication. From left to right: President Myles Brand, Dick Enberg. Photograph by IU Photographic Services. Courtesy of IU Archives (P0042375).

1987–1988

The Department of Applied Health Science is awarded a $161,520 grant from the US Department of Education to train one hundred Indiana elementary and secondary school teachers as drug abuse prevention specialists, with James Crowe serving as Project Director. With additional funding received for drug abuse prevention and education, Indiana University and the Monroe County community receive more funds under the Drug-Free Schools and Communities Act, per capita, than any other area in the country.

Hilltop Garden and Nature Center receives the National Gardening Association's Green Medal Award, recognizing it as one of the top ten youth gardens in America.

Hilltop Garden and Nature Center, 1993. The building was constructed and dedicated in 1993. Courtesy of IU Archives (P0033755).

1988–1989

Dean Mobley institutes a formal faculty exchange program between the School of HPER and the Beijing Institute of Physical Education and Sport in China (later renamed Beijing Sport University).

1989–1990

The name of the Department of Physical Education is changed to the Department of Kinesiology in recognition of its broader mission in the study of exercise physiology, biomechanics, motor development, modern dance, physical fitness, sports management, and other related areas.

Youth Programs at Hilltop Garden and Nature Center, June 1992. Courtesy of IU Archives (P0033749).

John M. Cooper working with scientific instruments, January 10, 1979. Photograph by IU News Bureau. Courtesy of IU Archives (P0053051).

The construction of new human performance laboratories is completed in the space formerly occupied by the Wrubel Computing Center. The labs support research in motor learning/control, exercise physiology and biochemistry, psychobiology of exercise and sport, biomechanics, and physical fitness assessment.

The June 1990 volume of *Research & Creative Activity*, Indiana University Bloomington, features the research of several faculty members. Professor Jack Raglin published the article "Anxious Athletes"; Professor David Koceja, "Muscles, Aging, and Exercise"; Professor Jesus Dapena, "Human Body Mechanics"; Professor Wayne Miller, "The 'Non-Diet Diet' Doctor"; Professor Joel Stager, "Exploring the Effects of Exercise"; and Professor Janet Wallace, "Getting in Shape: Today, Tomorrow, and Forever."

1990–1991

International partnerships continue to grow and flourish:

• President Yang and delegates from the Beijing Institute of Physical Education visit the school and IU campus during the fall of 1990.

• The School of HPER and the Taiwan National College of Physical Education and Sports enter into a formal faculty exchange agreement.

• The School of HPER enters into a formal Agreement of Friendship and Cooperation with Victoria University of Technology-Footscray Campus (Australia). The agreement encompasses the provisions for teaching and research personnel exchange, student exchange, and books/reference materials exchange.

1991–1992

A faculty team consisting of Professors David Gallahue, Joel Stager, and Jeff Edwards attempts to climb Mount McKinley in May 1992 to study weight loss and energy expenditure in low oxygen environments, the results of which can provide insights into cardio-respiratory diseases. Although stormy weather keeps them from reaching the 20,320-foot summit and high winds, sub-zero temperatures, and deep snow further challenged the expedition, the story grips the community and represents an extraordinary moment in the school's history.

(below) Dean Mobley shaking hands with then President of Beijing University of Physical Education (BUPE) at the formal partnership signing ceremony at BUPE, 1989. Former presidents and delegates were in attendance. Mrs. Betty Mobley is seated to the left of Dean Mobley. Courtesy of IU Archives (P0053111).

David Gallahue. Photograph by IU Photographic Services. Courtesy of IU Archives (P0053055).

Joel Stager, March 8, 1990. Photograph by IU News Bureau. Courtesy of IU Archives (P0053090).

The Department of Recreation and Park Administration finalizes a cooperative agreement with the National Park Service that establishes the National Center on Accessibility in January 1992, housed at Bradford Woods. Gary Robb is Director of the project and Edward Hamilton serves as Research Director.

1992–1993

In October 1992, the Department of Recreation and Park Administration makes application to the National Council on Accreditation for reaccreditation of its academic programs in Leisure Services Management, Natural Resources Recreation Management, and Therapeutic Recreation. The department's accreditation status at that time is one of the oldest and longest for professional preparation in these areas. The reaccreditation on-site visit takes place in November 1993.

1993–1994

HPER Dimensions is instituted as a new outlet for providing annual school news to alumni and friends.

The Department of Applied Health Science and the Institute for Drug Abuse Prevention hold a month-long commemoration of the thirtieth anniversary of the first *Surgeon General's Report on Smoking and Health* from mid-January to mid-February 1994. Lectures, symposia, forums, panel discussions, and other events commemorate this landmark event. The Honorable Joycelyn Elders, MD, Surgeon General of the United States, delivers a distinguished lecture on the Bloomington campus as part of the commemoration.

1994–1995

The Department of Applied Health Science is recognized by the State of Indiana as an "Approved Training Institution" for coursework leading to certification as an emergency medical technician.

The Department of Recreation and Park Administration receives the US Forest Service Wilderness Excellence Award for a two-year research and service initiative designed to educate and evaluate middle school teachers and their students on the local Charles C. Deam Wilderness.

1995–1996

The School of HPER celebrates its Golden Anniversary.

A new Academic Endowment Campaign is in development.

School of Health, Physical Education, and Recreation (formerly Men's Gymnasium, 1917). Photograph by IU Photographic Services. Courtesy of IU Archives (P0042370).

4

Years of Fulfillment and Transition

IN HIS FOREWORD TO THE SUMMER 1997 ISSUE OF *HPER Dimensions*, Dean Tony Mobley spoke to the success of the fiftieth anniversary celebration of the school and to the coming years. He noted that the nation was "in the midst of a fundamental cultural change":

> There has never been a greater interest in safe and healthful living, leisure lifestyles, fitness and sport, and the overall quality of life that is supported by healthy lifestyles. The best estimates we can find indicate that Americans spend more than $350 billion a year in the fitness, sport, and leisure market. The Dean further stated that as we build the bridge to the next century, our opportunities are boundless, limited only by our own initiative. Our goal is to seize this heightened interest in our professions and use it to improve the quality of life for all citizens. To do this, we reinforce our commitment to provide outstanding classroom and field experiences for our students, to serve our thousands of alumni, and to conduct research that is essential to the progress of the HPER fields.

The Dean's message was intended to encourage HPER students, faculty, and professionals to recognize the importance of the roles they have in shaping healthy lifestyles and quality of life. Mobley stressed, "We must rededicate ourselves to preparing visionary leaders for our professions and building a bridge to the future."

While savoring the accomplishments of the school's first fifty years, the 1990s presented new challenges and opportunities. America was becoming a recognizably multicultural society, the digital age was taking hold, and the economy was globalizing. If the world was becoming "flat," as one pundit put it, America was becoming fat. The nation's increasingly sedentary population was growing obese and prone to chronic diseases like never

(facing) Associate Dean of HPER Ruth Russell and IU President Myles Brand at the HPER Fiftieth Anniversary Reception and Dinner. Photograph by IU Photographic Services and Guy Zimmer. Courtesy of IU Archives (P0053245).

before. At the same time, all corners of society were hustling to keep up with an astonishing rate of scientific and technological advancement. The rapid pace of change was reflected in the instructional and research activities within the university, including the activities and initiatives in the school. Students and faculty alike were grappling with shifts in the nature of higher education. The turbulence in the 1990s could be considered the herald of changes to come in the HPER professions and degree programs of the school, and eventually, in the very structure of the school itself. Growing concerns over fitness and health, chronic disease, quality of life, population change, international partnerships, and the teaching/learning enterprise were front and center in the consciousness of the school.

The traditional classroom faded quickly as faculty embraced new technologies, ushering in new challenges for both students and teachers. The World Wide Web coupled with the emergence of digital technology opened new frontiers for innovation and experimentation. Projects aimed at taking advantage of new technology and tools in the classroom were on the rise. In the Department of Recreation and Park Administration, for example, students were introduced to a hypertext-based software program, HPERIntern, to help them navigate the process of finding and fulfilling their internship requirements. Not only was information better organized and easier to retrieve, but students also were guided through questions and processes such as resume preparation, writing goals and objectives, and cover-letter preparation on their own time and within a user-friendly framework.

Along with the application of technology to the teaching and learning process came an explosion in the use of technologies to promote online learning and distance education. In pursuit of cutting-edge technology, Kathleen Gilbert from the Department of Applied Health Science developed a new internet-based course called Grief in the Family Context. Gilbert utilized

email for class interaction in the beginning and added online conferencing as the class grew. Students read their assignments and posted responses, which enabled them to interact and exchange ideas with each other, the professor, and others who were involved with the course. The course was enthusiastically received by students and demonstrated a new venue for enhancing the delivery of HPER courses to students who could not be on campus to take courses.

By January 1999, the school had adopted a new strategic plan to guide it into the next century, *Living Well through Healthy Lifestyles*. Each of the school's departments and the Division of Recreational Sports outlined programs and academic areas that addressed the message of "living well." The Department of Applied Health Science promoted five academic areas that directly affected health and living well: health education and health promotion, human development and family studies, nutrition and dietetics, public health, and occupational safety. The Department of Kinesiology targeted living well through teaching education, athletic training, sport marketing and management, and exercise science. Programs in the Department of Recreation and Park Administration promoted living well through therapeutic recreation, outdoor recreation and resource management, parks and recreation, tourism, and recreational sport management. Finally, with new state-of-the-art facilities, the Division of Recreational Sports provided a full program of activities to promote living well among the twenty-five thousand students served by the division, as well as the academic and research missions of the school.

Across the school, research and professional services on issues and topics that directly influenced living well were addressed through a constellation of laboratories, centers, and institutes. For example, the Indiana Prevention Resource Center (IPRC), which was established in 1987 to assist Indiana-based prevention practitioners, unveiled a Veterans Resources Search

Engine in 2009–2010 that was designed to link veterans with national, regional, and state resources dealing directly with health and quality-of-life needs. The IPRC's purview was expanding in order to meet emerging problems. For example, by 2012, the institute included problem gambling prevention, as well as alcohol, tobacco, and other drug treatment, in its growing portfolio.

In the Motor Control Laboratory, David Koceja and his colleagues were investigating the balance and posture of older adults. A five-year $516,000 grant from the National Institute on Aging launched a significant study into the number one problem that compromises the ability to living well among the elderly, namely, falls. As the older population was rapidly expanding, with significant implications for health care and the potential for living well in old age, this research agenda was very important. Based on an improved understanding of the mechanisms responsible for balance, the research team could then focus on interventions to improve posture and balance.

The school moved forward on the activities outlined in the new strategic plan, drawing on momentum from the huge success of the Bloomington Endowment Campaign. Creating new faculty positions was an important piece in positioning the school to fulfill its living-well agenda. From the gifts totaling close to $5 million, these faculty chairs and professorships were just a few of the newly funded positions:

- Tony and Betty Mobley Professorship to support scholarly and professional activities in the areas of comprehensive wellness and health enhancement

- Child Development Professorship

- Patricia and Joel Meier Outdoor Leadership Chair

- L. J. and Faye E. Burrus Chair

- William L. Yarber Professorship in Health Education

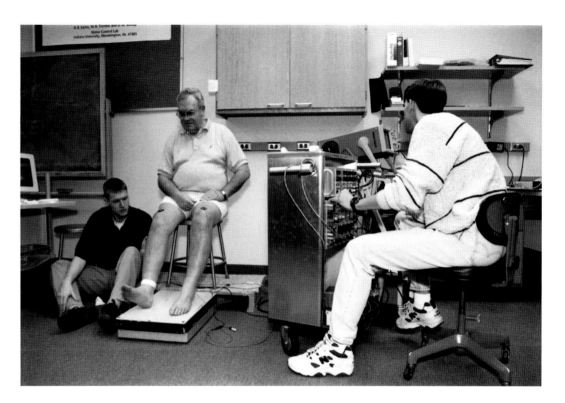

HPER Motor Performance Laboratory, February 26, 1997. Photograph by IU Photographic Services and Nick Judy. Courtesy of IU Archives (P0042380).

Dean Mobley was pleased to report in *HPER Dimensions*:

The campaign has already exceeded its initial goal for the School of HPER, and we look forward to an exceptionally successful campaign supported by loyal friends and alumni. This may be the most important recent program to the future development of the school.

The school is indebted to John Ross and Susie Bair as its first dedicated fundraisers, as well as to an exceptionally active HPER Alumni Board. By 2005, the school assembles its first Dean's Associates (renamed Dean's Alliance in 2013) under the leadership of Dean Gallahue, which further enhances the importance of private giving in the school.

With more than fourteen thousand alumni of the school plus an annual graduation number of more than six hundred degrees, the school's resources and gift giving provide evidence of past successes and future promise as a leader in promoting health, well-being, and quality of life for citizens and communities around the world.

The New Century: Move, Grow, and Change

For many, the first decade of the twenty-first century was a time of great anxiety. Terror and unrest gripped the nation with the bombing of the USS *Cole* in 2000 followed by the historic events of September 11, 2001: the hijacked airliner attacks on the World Trade Center and the Pentagon. For the first time in US history, all civilian air traffic ceased for three days. The anthrax attacks, which began one week later, killed five people and sickened seventeen and exacerbated fears of further terrorism. Most Americans had a sense that life as they had known it had changed forever.

Americans were further alarmed by what appeared to be increasing numbers of violent acts and other challenges to public health. Sustained growth in obesity rates and generalized social unrest were just two of the troublesome trends affecting the nation's health. A downturn in the academic performance of the nation's youth further added to a time of growing apprehension. While the use of technology in the classroom continued to advance at an exponential rate, the actual learning outcomes of students were troubling.

The school response to the times during the term of Dean David Gallahue could be summed up in the slogan "grow, move, and change." The school refocused attention on heightened concerns regarding individual health, the explosive growth in chronic diseases, increasing local and global unrest, and declines in the quality of life in communities around the country. School of HPER faculty and professional staff responded by developing targeted initiatives, innovative research, and new courses and degree programs and by adding new international partnerships. The opportunity to broaden the HPER platform into the public health frontier emerged as a logical and functional growth strategy. The school embraced the idea of a transition to a School of Public Health as an opportunity to lead in the creation of a new model for meeting the health and quality-of-life needs of the country's citizens and communities.

The academic year 2006–2007 brought the sixtieth anniversary year of the founding of the School of HPER, with a yearlong schedule of activities. In a speech to mark the occasion, IU Chancellor Kenneth R. R. Gros Louis noted that since the first doctorate was earned in 1948, the school had granted more than 7,200 graduate degrees. The school's maturation was reflected

HPER on the Wall

In 2004, after fifty-eight years of autonomous operation, the School of HPER had its crest mounted alongside those of the other IU schools in the entrance foyer of Bryan Hall, the main administrative building on the Bloomington campus. The installation event for the carved limestone crest recognized the school's place within the university, as well as its sustained excellence in teaching, research, and service.

HPER crest insignia, designed by Marjorie Rash Miller (BS in Nursing, 1958; MS in Health Education, 1969). Courtesy of IU School of Public Health–Bloomington.

HPER crest on the wall in the foyer of Bryan Hall. Courtesy of IU School of Public Health–Bloomington.

Controversy over Naming of Wildermuth Intramural Center

In his report to the Board of Trustees meeting in May 2007, President Adam Herbert cited the recent public controversy about former trustee Ora Wildermuth and the building that bears his name, the Wildermuth Intramural Center. The controversy surfaced after *Indiana Daily Student* (*IDS*) columnist Andrew Shaffer questioned the naming of the building for an individual—Judge Ora Wildermuth, a former trustee—who was known to be against racial integration. President Herbert announced that he had appointed a special committee to study the matter.

In October 2008, a recommendation was made to change the name to the William L. Garrett–Ora L. Wildermuth Fieldhouse. Garrett was IU's first black basketball player, at a time when black players were barred from the Big Ten by unspoken consensus. Following Garrett's addition to the IU team, African American players were recruited by coaches around the country. In February 2009,

the *IDS* reported that the name had been changed to the William L. Garrett–Ora L. Wildermuth Intramural Center; however, the name was never officially changed, as the Board of Trustees confirmed in February 2009.

The building has generated other controversies over the years. For example, in November 2013, students once again raised objections, this time to the tiles in the front hallways of the Wildermuth Intramural Center. Among the tiles was one that appeared to be a swastika, a symbol associated with the Nazis. The symbol, however, actually represented a sacred Hindu symbol meaning good fortune or well-being, which was popular at the time it was installed. While the complaining student suggested that the university remove all tiles containing the symbol, the trustees wisely saw the issue as a teachable moment, preferring to inform visitors and students as to the history and true meaning of the symbol.

---

not only in high enrollments and alumni but also in the substantially increased faculty productivity and external funding. Additionally, since its founding in 1974, the Division of Recreational Sports had achieved national recognition as the best collegiate recreational sports program in the nation. Gros Louis also noted that HPER had remained "innovative, creative, young."

Perhaps it is such a unique combination of freshness and maturity that should most be celebrated in HPER. . . . The special spirit of the School is as vibrant now as it was in the efflorescent period of which Wells spoke, but also mark the successes that require 60 years.

Among the events of the year was a visit by Acting Surgeon General Kenneth P. Moritsugu in November, during which he delivered a speech titled Prevention is the Real Cure. Indiana State Health Commissioner Judy Monroe, MD, also gave a lecture during the year titled Tackling Public Health Enemy #1: Tobacco. Among the other presentations given during the year was David Compton's Sedentary Living and Morbidity in America: The Warrant for Transforming Public Parks and Recreation Agencies. The messages during the sixtieth-anniversary year punctuated growing concerns and issues related to health and quality of life.

In the fall semester of 2006, the school recorded 1,802 undergraduate and 333 graduate student majors, for a total of 2,135, which represented a 709-percent increase since the founding of the school. On June 30, 2007, a total of 809 degrees and certificates were conferred, as compared with the 61 degrees awarded in June 1947. Total credit-hour production for the school in 2006–2007 was 83,834. Since the school's founding, the faculty had diversified and grown considerably. In 2007, there were thirty-eight emeriti faculty members, sixty-five full-time faculty, seventeen lecturers, eight visiting lecturers, four academic specialists, an assistant scientist, a visiting scientist, fifteen research associates, and sixteen visiting research associates. By comparison, in 1946 Dean Patty reported thirty-three full-time faculty members, twelve part-time faculty members, and fourteen graduate assistants.

The Transition Begins

During the administration of Dean David Gallahue, then-Provost Michael McRobbie authorized a task force at Indiana University to determine the need for a school of public health in Indiana. The task force was cochaired by Distinguished IUB Professor Bernice Pescosolido and Indiana State Health Commissioner Judith Monroe. Other members of the task force included the Chair of the Department of Applied Health Science at the time, the Acting Chair of the Department of Public Health at IUPUI, and other faculty members. The task force recommended that such a school was indeed needed, given the critical public health issues facing the state and the nation. In 2007, Robert Goodman was appointed as the School of HPER's seventh dean, and he immediately undertook efforts to transition the school toward the eventual establishment of a school of public health on the Bloomington campus.

In May 2009, IU President Michael A. McRobbie issued a news release announcing a plan that called for the formation of two schools of public health in Indiana. Subsequently, HPER began the formal process of transitioning to a school of public health. This transition was part of the IU Public Health Initiative, which was launched in 2009 to address pressing public health needs across Indiana. This initiative called for establishing the state's only schools of public health, one at Indiana University-Purdue University Indianapolis and the other on the Bloomington campus. The formation of the Bloomington campus school would ultimately entail the transition of the School of HPER to the Indiana University School of Public Health–Bloomington. This transition provided the opportunity

Courtyard Transformation

At the meeting of the Board of Trustees in September 2008, the HPER Courtyard Project was presented and unanimously approved. Dean Robert Goodman was instrumental in the realization of this long-held dream for a better utilization of the space. This facility expansion came at an opportune moment, as the school was simultaneously beginning its transformation into the School of Public Health. The central courtyard of the HPER building was to be enclosed, and new offices, instructional and lab space, and an auditorium constructed. Groundbreaking on the Courtyard Project began in June 2010, after twenty years of hard work toward the development of the courtyard space. The project produced 28,000 square feet of new space, including a 174-seat auditorium, which was dedicated on October 11, 2011, as the Tony A. Mobley Auditorium, in honor of Dean Emeritus Mobley.

for traditional HPER disciplines to transform initiatives and achievements already in place into a new platform that widened the sphere of impact and influence.

At the Board of Trustees meeting in May 2009, President McRobbie reported that Indiana traditionally ranked very poorly in terms of major public health benchmarks and indicators of chronic diseases such as obesity, cardiovascular disease, and diabetes. A major step toward improving the health of Indiana citizens, McRobbie said, would be to have two strong and engaged public health schools to help identify effective responses to chronic disease and to promote healthier lifestyles. He reported that the school in Bloomington would be based at HPER, now the third-largest school on campus, and would focus on rural health issues, general wellness, and other areas that build on HPER's strengths. At IUPUI, the school would grow from the Department of Public Health in the School of Medicine, with a core mission directed toward urban public health. Planning on both campuses was to be overseen by a new IU Public Health Coordinating Council chaired by Edwin Marshall, Vice President for Diversity, Equity, and Multicultural Affairs, who was also a noted public health practitioner. At the completion of the university planning and approval phase, accreditation would be sought from the Council on Education for Public Health (CEPH). Accreditation would provide the opportunity for the professional qualification of the master's degree and enable the university to compete for specialized funding from agencies such as the CDCP.

On June 24, 2011, the Indiana University Board of Trustees approved key components of the IU Public Health Initiative, including a request to change the name of the School of Health, Physical Education, and Recreation to the Indiana University School of Public Health–Bloomington. The name change was to be enacted upon completion of presentations to the Indiana Commission for Higher Education and the CEPH. These actions

School of Health, Physical Education, and Recreation. Courtesy of IU School of Public Health–Bloomington.

by the Board of Trustees were seen as highly significant to Indiana's response to the public health challenges in the state.

President McRobbie interrupted the proceedings of the Board of Trustees meeting on October 14, 2011, to inform the trustees that the Indiana Commission for Higher Education had approved the proposals for two new schools of public health. On the same date, the Indiana Commission for Higher Education unanimously approved IU's request to rename the school. This endorsement represented the last one needed prior to submitting a formal application for accreditation by CEPH, the independent agency authorized by the US Department of Education to accredit schools of public health. As of July 2011, there were forty-eight CEPH-accredited schools of public health in the world.

School of Public Health Building. Courtesy of IU School of Public Health–Bloomington.

In its final year as the School of HPER, September 2011 to August 2012, the school awarded its last official degrees. Henceforth all degrees would be awarded by the IU School of Public Health–Bloomington. By the end, the School of HPER could boast of nearly twenty thousand alumni.

This volume has barely touched on the tremendous accomplishments made by the School of Health, Physical Education, and Recreation during its operations from July 1, 1946, through August 2012. The school's legacy of achievements is a testimony to its rich history and strong foundation, upon which the new Indiana University School of Public Health–Bloomington is being built.

WITH A CHANGING WORLD and critical national issues regarding health, wellness, and quality of life, the transition to the School of Public Health was a natural evolution for all the disciplines and professions historically served by the School of HPER. A public health foundation offered the opportunity to attain accreditation at the school level, heretofore not available for schools of health, physical education, and recreation. The name change to the IU School of Public Health–Bloomington also conveyed the addition of critical disciplines in epidemiology, biostatistics, environmental health, and health administration, enhancing the school's original mission of preventing disease, promoting health, and improving quality of life. As the School of HPER evolved, new frontiers were continually being opened; its transformation into the School of Public Health was both natural and strategic.

The formal naming ceremony of the IU School of Public Health–Bloomington was held on September 28, 2012, and marked a major milestone in the history of Indiana University. The historic event was held in the Tony A. Mobley Auditorium, in the newly constructed section of what had now become the School of Public Health building. The naming ceremony,

(above) IU President Michael McRobbie speaking at the School of Public Health naming ceremony, September 28, 2012. Photograph by IU Communications. Courtesy of IU School of Public Health–Bloomington.

(left) Dean Mohammad Torabi, Provost and Executive Vice President Lauren Robel, and President Michael McRobbie unveil the new School of Public Health sign at the naming ceremony, September 28, 2012. Photograph by IU Communications and Christopher Meyer. Courtesy of IU School of Public Health–Bloomington.

School of Public Health naming ceremony, September 28, 2012. Photograph by IU Communications. Courtesy of IU School of Public Health–Bloomington.

School of Public Health naming ceremony, September 28, 2012. From left to right: Dean Emeritus Tony Mobley, Dr. David Lohrmann, Dr. Bryan McCormick, Dr. David Koceja, Dean Emeritus David Gallahue. Photograph by IU Communications and Christopher Meyer. Courtesy of IU School of Public Health–Bloomington.

presided over by President Michael McRobbie, was attended by Trustee Patrick Shoulders, long-serving member of the board, Trustee Philip Eskew, Jr., Vice Chair of the Board of Trustees, Provost Lauren Robel, Vice President Edwin Marshall, and Interim Dean Mohammad Torabi. Other dignitaries included emeriti Deans Tony Mobley and David Gallahue. The auditorium was filled with visitors, faculty, staff, and students. The event marked an important transition and the start of a new vision for the future of the school. Indiana University was now positioned to address the most pressing health needs of individuals, communities, and the nation via a platform that commanded a wider sphere of influence. It was the dawn of new hopes for expanded models for both the traditional HPER professions and the traditional foundations of public health.

Highlights from the Era, 1996–2013

1996–1997

Charles Beeker, with a team of researchers, discovers a trove of artifacts from the Taino culture in the Caribbean sinkhole Manantial de la Aleta, off the coast of the Dominican Republic. All recovered artifacts are transported within twenty-four hours to the headquarters of the National Park of the East and the El Faro a Colón Museum in Santo Domingo.

The Department of Recreation and Park Administration has a distance education network of eleven sites throughout the Indiana Higher Education Telecommunication System.

1997–1998

The Master of Public Health is fully accredited by the Council on Education for Public Health for a five-year period. The following courses are offered for the first time: (a) Health Care in the Minority Community, (b) Violence Prevention in American Society, (c) International Health and Social Issues, (d) Health and Surviving the College Years, (e) Stress Prevention and Management, (f) Grief in the Family Context, and (g) Nutrient and Gene Expression.

1998–1999

The National Center on Accessibility receives more than $300,000 in contracts for the study and implementation of accessibility programs for the National Park Service.

1999–2000

Seventeen Indiana communities share in a $7.5-million grant to the Indiana Prevention Resource Center, awarded by the US Center for Substance Abuse Prevention for the creation of grassroots prevention coalitions to reduce alcohol, tobacco, and other drug-related problems.

2000–2001

The doctoral program in the Department of Applied Health Science is ranked number one in the nation by the *Journal of Health Education*, and the department's Master of Public Health is ranked eleventh nationally by *US News and World Report*.

2001–2002

The school has cooperative agreements with seventeen international institutions.

The Department of Kinesiology is ranked number one in research productivity among the Big Ten institutions at a meeting of Big Ten deans and directors.

2002–2003

The nationally recognized Division of Recreational Sports wins top National Intramural-Recreational Sports Association awards for its 2002–2003 marketing campaign, GETAWAY, which promoted the benefits of participation in recreational sports.

A new school-wide course, T142 Living Well, is developed to represent the school's commitment to the promotion of living well.

2003–2004

On February 6, 2004, the Eighteenth Annual Girls and Women in Sports Day, Title IX: Outcomes and Opportunities, is held on the Bloomington campus sponsored by the School of HPER and the School of Law. Birch Bayh, eighteen-year-veteran US Senator, IU School of Law graduate, and principal author of Title IX, participates on a discussion panel as part of the day's activities.

The Board of Trustees approves the renaming of the graduate program in Kinesiology as the John M. Cooper Kinesiology Program in honor of their long-time colleague who changed the way kinesiology is taught in the United States.

The Clinical Exercise Physiology master's degree program achieves the highest mark of excellence from the American College of Sports Medicine. Indiana University is one of only five universities to achieve this status.

The Department of Recreation and Park Administration is named one of the top 3 out of more than 250 such programs in the United States by the Council on Accreditation. The department celebrates the successful continuation of twenty-five years of accreditation while receiving approval for a master's degree in Tourism Management.

In 2003, the Department of Applied Science PhD program in Health Behavior is ranked number one in the nation among nonschools of public health and fifth among all schools offering health education and doctoral degrees.

2004–2005

The Department of Kinesiology reinstates its Dance Program for majors, which had been put on moratorium in 1991. The department also expands its Sport Marketing and Management degree program.

2005–2006

As part of the Life Sciences Initiative on campus, President Adam Herbert requests that the School of HPER create a plan for a university-wide health and wellness program.

The Division of Recreational Sports serves over 1.8 million participants in self-directed use of facilities; personal trainers conduct 3,133 personal training sessions; and there are 21,946 participants in intramural sports.

2006–2007

Two new labs are established in the Department of Applied Health Science: the Applied Health Behavior Research Laboratory, and the Industrial Hygiene Laboratory.

A new Center for Minority Health is established in the Department of Applied Health Science for the promotion of research, outreach, programming, and training related to health disparities.

The name of the Department of Recreation and Park Administration is officially changed to the Department of Recreation, Park, and Tourism Studies.

2007–2008

The IU Contemporary Dance Program performs numerous events throughout the year, ending with ever-popular *Hammer and Nail* concert, a collaboration between HPER and the Jacobs School of Music.

Modern Dance, June 2007. Courtesy of IU School of Public Health–Bloomington.

The Department of Applied Health Science develops two new research centers: the Center for Sexual Health Promotion, directed by Michael Reece, and the Heartland Safety and Health Education Center, led by Senior Lecturer Cheryl Holmes.

A national conference titled *Obesity: Causes, Consequences, and Policy Challenges* is held on the IU campus with coordination provided by faculty in the Department of Applied Health Science.

2008–2009

Hilltop Garden and Nature Center is administratively transferred out of the School of HPER.

John Seffrin, former Chair of the Department of Applied Health Science and current CEO of the American Cancer Society, is awarded an Honorary Doctor of Science at the IU Bloomington Winter Commencement held on December 20, 2008.

2009–2010

As part of HPER's transition to the School of Public Health, new doctoral degrees in epidemiology and environmental health receive approval by the Board of Trustees.

The national *Journal of Sexual Medicine* devotes an entire issue to reporting the results of the National Survey of Sexual Health and Behavior conducted by the Center for Sexual Health Promotion.

2010–2011

A spring storm on May 25 causes major damage around the city of Bloomington and on the IU campus. The area around the School of HPER was one of the hardest hit, with over thirty-five trees lost and wind causing major damage to fencing and grounds.

2011–2012

The Indiana Commission on Higher Education approves a PhD in Epidemiology and a PhD in Environmental Health.

The IU Board of Trustees approves the new Department of Epidemiology and Biostatistics at its February 2012 meeting. Four new faculty are hired, and Professor Ka He is hired as the department chair. The department offers the MPH and PhD degrees in Epidemiology and the MPH in Biostatistics.

The approved new Department of Environmental Health focuses on the human health effects of environmental triggers. The department includes Professor James Klaunig serving as Chair, Associate Professors Lisa Kamendulis and Barbara Hocevar, and Clinical Assistant Professor Joanna Shimek. The program is the first in the state of Indiana to offer a PhD in Environmental Health, with enrolled graduate students at both the MPH and PhD levels for the fall semester of 2011.

Transition Milestones in 2012

JANUARY 7 - School of Public Health Accreditation Self-Study Steering Committee initiates the SPH accreditation self-study.

JANUARY 23 - Staff are formally updated on the status of the transition and accreditation.

FEBRUARY 7 - Faculty are formally updated on the status of the transition and accreditation.

FEBRUARY 9 - Graduate Data Management Working-Group is convened.

FEBRUARY 13 - Centers and Institutes Working-Group is convened.

FEBRUARY 16 - Evaluation and Competency Assessment Working-Group is convened.

FEBRUARY 16 - Student Affairs Working-Group is convened.

FEBRUARY 17 - Workforce Development Working-Group is convened.

MARCH 8 - Kathleen Miner, Emory University's Rollins School of Public Health Associate Dean, meets as an external consultant with select members of the central administration and school faculty and staff regarding the transition progress to date.

APRIL 26 - Faculty approve a revised school constitution and new by-laws.

JUNE 23 - The Council on Education for Public Health accepts the application for the Indiana University School of Public Health–Bloomington, thus signaling the initiation of accreditation procedures.

JULY 18 - The Association of Schools of Public Health grants associate membership to Indiana University School of Public Health–Bloomington.

Post-transition Accomplishments

- In 2011–2012, the school expands its efforts in career services and advising, as reflected in the hire of a full-time Director of Career Services. Under the new Director's leadership, the SPH Office of Career Services launches several new programs and initiatives. In 2013–2014 alone, the office experienced a total student engagement of 4,746 interactions spanning from the fall 2013 semester through early April 2014.

- The school sees an increase of 47.9 percent in faculty research publications from 2011 to 2013.

- The number of new research proposals submitted to extramural entities rises impressively from 2011 to 2013.

- In 2012–2013, the school's total credit-hour production sets a record at 93,490.

- In 2012–2013, 2,225 undergraduates are enrolled in the School of Public Health–Bloomington.

- In 2012–2013, 259 master's degree students are enrolled in the School of Public Health–Bloomington.

- In 2012–2013, 133 doctoral degree students are enrolled in the School of Public Health–Bloomington.

- In 2012–2013, the school is the third-largest unit on the Bloomington campus in terms of both enrollment and credit hours.

- In 2012–2013, 161 international students major in school programs, constituting 6.2 percent of all school majors. Forty-two students are from China; thirty-five students are from South Korea.

- In 2012–2013, 102 School of Public Health–Bloomington students study in international locations, an increase of 60 percent from the last report generated by IU's Office of Overseas Studies.

- In 2012–2013, technology and new forms of pedagogy gain increasingly important roles in the life of both the school and the university. A Director of Online Education is hired to provide leadership in this area.

School of Public Health sign.
Courtesy of IU School of Public Health–Bloomington.

- In 2012–2013, the school's Office of Global and Community Health Partnerships continues to spearhead efforts in community engagement and workforce development. In that year, 222 continuing education events are delivered to over 16,000 members of the public health workforce. A total of 757 professionals in Indiana work directly with faculty on School of Public Health–Bloomington initiatives. In addition, sixty-two faculty and staff work with over ninety-four international partners.

- The school receives thirty-six external awards that total $5,008,520, an increase of approximately 10 percent from the previous year.

- In early 2013, the school receives $1,289,074.48 in private gifts, compared to $369,850.79 at the same time in the previous year.

- During the 2013 spring semester, 381 students apply for 83 privately funded scholarships that totaled over $145,000.

- In 2013, the hire of an Assistant Dean for Student Academic Affairs signals greater efforts toward dedicated and broader approaches to addressing student-related issues and services within the school.

- In 2013–2014, the school expands its efforts to support diversity and minority recruitment, as reflected in the hire of a Director of Student Diversity and Inclusion.

5

On the Shoulders of Legends

INDIANA UNIVERSITY SCHOOL OF HEALTH, PHYSICAL EDUCATION, AND RECREATION, now the IU School of Public Health–Bloomington, has enjoyed pioneering and visionary leaders who provided critical leadership throughout the school's history, from its early roots to the present. The deans who have led the school represent the highest level of professional achievement and leadership expertise, from which the university and the state have greatly benefited. As the school embraces its future, the legacy upon which it builds is strong, well-established, and highly recognized as the best in the country. This legacy is due, in part, to the fact that the university has chosen well the deans and faculty members of the school.

(facing) Sample Gates in the spring. Courtesy of IU Communications.

WILLARD WALTER PATTY, First Dean of the School of Health, Physical Education, and Recreation (1946–1957)

On the recommendation of President Herman B Wells, W. W. Patty was appointed by the IU Board of Trustees as the first Dean of the School of HPER, on July 1, 1946. It is noteworthy that the first Dean of HPER represented the health profession. Patty began his career at IU in 1925. In the 1930s, Patty initiated a program of extension-like classes in health, physical education, and recreation that he and others conducted throughout the state.

In 1931, the Department of Physical Welfare Training was established in the School of Education with emphases in health, hygiene, physical education, coaching, recreation, safety, and public health nursing. President William Bryan recommended that Professor Patty be given the titles of Director of the Physical Welfare Training Department of the School of Education and Director of the Normal College of the American Gymnastic Union of Indiana University. Patty was known as a determined and persistent leader, especially in bringing about the creation of the School of HPER.

By agreement with the Indiana University Board of Trustees, Patty established all of the degree programs in the school: the Bachelor of Science, Master of Science, director, and doctoral degrees in each of the three fields of Health and Safety, Physical Education, and Recreation. Among his many accomplishments, Dean Patty served as President of the Indiana Health Council. He also served as associate editor for three national journals: *Research Quarterly, Journal of Health and Physical Education,* and *School Activities Magazine.*

The June 1957 issue of the HPER Alumni Newsletter paid tribute to Dean Patty upon his retirement:

Willard W. Patty, March 1941. Courtesy of IU Archives (P0021592).

After 32 years as a member of the faculty at IU, W. W. Patty is retiring as Dean of the School of HPER. Patty has been a pioneer in HPER in Indiana. He has been instrumental in laying the foundation for professional fields in the local area as well as in the nation. His continued interest and efforts have aided greatly the growth of professional organizations. From the time of his appointment as Director of the Welfare Training Department at IU, he has worked unselfishly for the growth and status of the department concerned with health, physical education, and recreation. His efforts were climaxed by the formation of the School of HPER in 1946 and by the formation of specialized programs and degrees in HPER. In addition to his duties as Dean of HPER, he served admirably as Director of Athletics for more than a year until that position was filled. Patty's connection with the professional organizations in the community, the state, and the nation will be felt for a long time. He has laid a foundation for future growth.

ARTHUR S. DANIELS (1957–1966)

Arthur Daniels was appointed Dean on July 1, 1957. Prior to coming to Indiana University, Daniels coached football and directed intramurals as an assistant professor at Allegheny College (1931–1932) and was an associate professor on the graduate faculty at the University of Illinois (1937–1945). He then became Professor of Physical Education at Ohio State University (1947–1957).

Early in his term, Dean Daniels commissioned a ten-year master plan for the school. As a result, new standards for the graduate programs were successfully implemented, including new admission standards, screening instruments to reduce the

Arthur Daniels, December 15, 1957. Photograph by IU Photographic Services. Courtesy of IU Archives (P0026766).

number of borderline students, and the requirements for doctoral candidacy, which culminated in qualifying examinations.

Considered a dean of high standards, Daniels led by example as head of the flourishing new school and in other professional leadership positions. He served as President of the American Association for Health, Physical Education, and Recreation (AAHPER) in 1961. The AAHPER had grown to nearly twenty-six thousand members by this time. Daniels also held membership on the Educational Policies Commission of the National Education Association. Among other honors and awards, Daniels was Life Member and Honor Fellow of the AAHPER; Fellow and member of the Board of Trustees of the American College of Sports Medicine; Fellow of the American Academy of Physical Education; a member of Board of Governors, Riley Memorial Association; and Consultant to the President's Council on Youth Fitness.

One of the early contributors to the school's history of leadership in adapted education, Daniels was the author of one of the first textbooks in the field. In 1965, Dean Daniels and Professor Janet MacLean coauthored seven articles for the *International Encyclopedia of Sports Medicine*.

In 1964, Dean Daniels completed a successful trip to Hong Kong and Taiwan for the US State Department, during which he was acting on an advisory and intermediary basis to help establish closer contacts between IU and universities/colleges in these regions. His final report was enthusiastically accepted by both the US State Department and officials in Hong Kong and Taiwan.

JOHN ENDWRIGHT (1966–1975)

John Endwright's first appointment was as an instructor in the Department of Physical Education for Men in 1948. The next year, he was given the additional title of Administrative Assistant to the Dean. In 1957, he became Assistant Professor and Assistant Dean of the school. In 1965, he was promoted to Associate Professor and Associate Dean. Endwright worked closely with the dean's office, and following the untimely death of Dean Daniels, he was appointed Acting Dean and Chair of the Department of Physical Education for Men effective July 1, 1966. He was appointed as Dean of the school on November 1, 1967, and served in this capacity until 1975.

John Endwright, October 3, 1967. Photograph by IU Photographic Services. Courtesy of IU Archives (P0029888).

Upon relinquishing his position as Dean in 1975, Professor Endwright assumed a teaching position in the Department of Physical Education and accepted the positions of Coordinator of College and University Placement for the school and Coordinator of Alumni Relations. Dean Endwright's professional involvements included serving as chair of a number of state, Midwest, and national committees. His most notable position was that of national Chair of the Deans and Directors Council of the American Association for Health, Physical Education, and Recreation. He also served as an editorial consultant for several publishing companies in the evaluation of manuscripts. He received an Honor Award from the Indiana Association for Health, Physical Education, and Recreation for his accomplishments.

John Endwright devoted his entire professional career to administration, teaching, and counseling. He always maintained an open door policy, with constant availability to students and colleagues. His era as dean was characterized by kindness, fairness, and common sense.

ANITA ALDRICH (1975–1976)

Anita Aldrich was appointed Chair and Professor of the Department of Physical Education for Women and Professor of Education in 1964. Upon the retirement of Dean Endwright, she was appointed as Acting Dean, a position she held until the appointment of Tony Mobley as Dean on July 1, 1976. Upon the merger of the Departments of Physical Education for Men and Women in 1977, Aldrich assumed the position of Chair for the new Department of Physical Education.

Aldrich was a pioneer in curriculum development. During the 1960s, she served on the President's Council on Physical Fitness and as a member of the Advisory Committee of the Educational Policies Commission. In 1965–1966, Aldrich received a grant from the US Commissioner of Education to support

Anita Aldrich, May 14, 1971. Photograph by IU Photographic Services. Courtesy of IU Archives (P0020571).

long-term research to identify and evaluate a conceptual framework for the curriculum in physical education for kindergarten through the bachelor's degree. In the same year, Anita Aldrich served as chair of the local planning committee for the Workshop in Physical Education for the Mentally Retarded, which was funded by the Joseph P. Kennedy, Jr., Foundation and the American Alliance for Health, Physical Education, Recreation, and Dance (AAHPERD).

Aldrich served as president of the Missouri Association for Health, Physical Education, and Recreation; president of the Central District of the AAHPERD; and president of the AAHPERD. She was a member of the Education Policies Commission of the National Education Association and in 1961 was appointed advisor to President John F. Kennedy's Fitness Council.

Aldrich was a member of steering committees for the physical education curriculum guide *Motion and Direction* and for a Lilly Foundation study to determine the physical competencies of elementary school children. Most notably, she became the first woman member of the Indiana University Athletics Committee in 1971 and, after serving seven years, was named the first woman to chair this committee, a position she held from 1978 until her retirement in 1985.

Aldrich received many honors and recognitions throughout her career. Among them were the Distinguished Alumni Achievement Award from the University of Missouri–Kansas City; the Leadership Recognition Award from the Indiana Association for Health, Physical Education, Recreation, and Dance; the Honor Award from the AAHPERD; and the Outstanding Service in the Advancement of Athletics Award from the Athletic Institute. She was named an Honor Fellow of the AAHPERD and was elected to the American Academy of Physical Education. In 1979–1980, she received the Recognition Award for Promotion of Growth and Attainment of Goals of Women's Athletics at Indiana University. She was inducted into the IU Intercollegiate Athletics Hall of Fame in 1996.

TONY MOBLEY (1976–2002)

Prior to coming to Indiana University as Dean of the School of HPER, Tony Mobley held a faculty appointment at Western Illinois University, where he established a department of recreation, of which he became chair in 1968. While at Western he also assisted in the development of the School of Health, Physical Education, and Recreation, where Harry Fritz, an IU alumnus, served as the first Dean. In 1972, Mobley accepted a position at Pennsylvania State University, where he served as the Chair of the Department of Recreation and Parks.

During 1970–1971, Mobley was selected to serve as a Fellow in the Academic Administration Internship Program of the American Council on Education. This program involved in-depth training in university administration. His assignment primarily involved serving the offices of the chancellor and provost at North Carolina State University. Mobley's involvements in professional organizations were many. He was President of the Society of Park and Recreation Educators and of the NRPA. In 1981 he was given the highest honor bestowed by the park and recreation profession, the coveted National Distinguished Professional Award from the NRPA. Also, Dean Mobley and Professors Rey Carlson, Ted Deppe, and Janet MacLean were selected as Founding Fellows of the Academy of Leisure Sciences and of the Academy for Parks and Recreation Administration. Mobley also served as a trustee of the NRPA and as the first President of the NIFS, in 1986. Among Dean Mobley's many honors are J. B. Nash Scholar and Lecturer and from the AAHPERD the College and University Administrator's Council National Honor Award.

Upon his retirement after twenty-six years of leading the school, Dean Mobley had served as the longest-sitting dean in Indiana University history. An article in the 2002 *HPER Dimensions* noted other highlight from Mobley's career:

Under his leadership, the school had more than doubled its $4 million goal for the Bloomington Academic Endowment Campaign and built the state-of-the-art Student Recreational Sports Center. . . . He expanded the school's visibility internationally, forging partnerships with 17 universities around the world. . . . He has received an array of distinctions including a listing in *Who's Who in America*; the R. Tait McKenzie Award from the American Alliance for Health, Physical Education, Recreation, and Dance; a Distinguished Fellow Award from the Society of Park and Recreation Educators . . . and a Sagamore of the Wabash award from the governor of Indiana for meritorious service.

During Tony Mobley's term as dean of the school:

• Enrollment in the school doubled and participation in Recreational Sports increased to twenty-seven thousand students per year;
• Research productivity, grants, and contracts increased dramatically;
• The Departments of Physical Education for Men and for Women merged into a single department, the Department of Kinesiology;
• Human Performance and Food Science Laboratories were constructed and put into operation;
• Income from fundraising grew from less than $20,000 per year to commitments of more than $9 million following the unparalleled success of the Academic Endowment Campaign;
• The school continuously ranked as one of the top schools in the country;
• Twenty-one faculty members served as presidents of fourteen national professional organizations;
• The number of alumni grew from 6,600 in 1976 to more than 16,000, representing all 50 states and 42 countries.

His was quite a legacy.

Tony Mobley, December 5, 1990. Photograph by IU News Bureau. Courtesy of IU Archives (P0053058).

David Gallahue, October 6, 1994. Photograph by IU Photographic Services. Courtesy of IU Archives (P0053054).

DAVID L. GALLAHUE (2002–2007)

Following thirty-two years on the faculty of the School of HPER, Professor David Gallahue was appointed dean in 2002. He came to this position having had many years of experience under the mentorship of Tony Mobley. Dean Gallahue's boundless energy and curiosity opened up many opportunities during his years on the faculty. He had served as Assistant Chair for the Department of Physical Education, Assistant Dean for Research and Development, and Coordinator of Continuing Education. He was Acting Dean while Dean Mobley was on sabbatical and Associate Dean for Academic Affairs and Research. By the completion of his deanship, the school had become the third-largest academic unit on the Bloomington campus; credit-hour production had increased by 21 percent; and funding for grants and contracts had increased 61 percent, to $5.2 million.

Dean Gallahue had a distinguished career as an expert in the motor development and movement skill learning of children and youth, particularly in physical activity and sport settings. He authored two major textbooks, *Understanding Motor Development: Infants, Children, Adolescents, Adults* and *Developmental Physical Education for All Children*. Over the course of his career, he spoke or taught at more than three hundred universities and conferences in more than twenty countries. His professional leadership roles included President of the National Association for Sport and Physical Education and Chair of the Council on Physical Education for Children. He survived a storm on Mount McKinley that killed ten climbers, and in May 2001 he led the Great Wall Walk, an event that brought together about seventy participants from the School of HPER and the Beijing Sport University. Among his honors and recognitions are a Healthy American Fitness Leader's Award and, from the Council on Physical Education for Children, the Distinguished Service Award.

ROBERT M. GOODMAN (2007–2010)

Robert M. Goodman succeeded David Gallahue in 2007 as the seventh Dean of the School of HPER. Prior to joining Indiana University, he served on the faculties of the University of South Carolina, the University of North Carolina, and Tulane University. He also directed the Center for Community Research at the Wake Forest University School of Medicine. Immediately prior to coming to IU, Goodman was Professor and Chair of the Department of Behavioral and Community Health Services in the Graduate School of Public Health at the University of Pittsburgh. Dean Goodman earned graduate degrees in public health from the University of Hawaii and the University of North Carolina. Fluent in Mandarin Chinese, he also earned a master's degree in East Asian history. He is a talented performer of both classical violin and fiddle music. His professional expertise focuses on community health development and programs, building community coalitions and capacity, evaluation methods, and organizational development. Goodman was the recipient of the 2004 Distinguished Fellow Award from the Society for Public Health Education, for which he has served as president.

With the role of life sciences strong on the campus and the state of Indiana's need for a school of public health, Dean Goodman recognized both the challenges and the exciting opportunities for the school in the areas of public health, health promotion, and quality of life for citizens and communities alike. He embraced the deanship at a time when there was heightened concern over the major health issues confronting the state and the nation. Dean Goodman began the process of exploring ways to grow the school's programs and increase its impact, which would lead to the creation of the School of Public Health. During his tenure, he was instrumental in realizing the long-held dream of adding office space and what would become the state-of-the-art Mobley Auditorium in the HPER building's inner courtyard area. In October 2010, Goodman stepped down as dean, remaining on the faculty as Professor of Applied Health Science.

Robert M. Goodman. Courtesy of IU School of Public Health–Bloomington.

MOHAMMAD R. TORABI, Eighth Dean of the School of HPER and Founding Dean of the School of Public Health–Bloomington (2010–present) (Chancellor's Professor and Professor of Applied Health Science, 1984–present)

Mohammad R. Torabi's first appointment at Indiana University was as Assistant Professor of Health and Safety Education, in 1984. In 1996, he assumed the position of Assistant Chair of the Department of Applied Health Science and in 1999 he became Chair of the Department of Applied Health Science and Director of the Center for Health and Safety Studies. By 2008, he had acquired the additional titles of Director (later Co-Director) of the Institute for Drug Abuse Prevention and Adjunct Professor of Public Health in the IU School of Medicine (IUPUI). On November 1, 2010, Torabi was appointed as Interim Dean, and upon the creation of the new Indiana University School of Public Health–Bloomington, in January 2012, he became its founding dean.

Torabi's educational preparation is in public health. He focused throughout his career on the measurement and evaluation of school and public health education programs, and his research extends into health promotion and key factors related to individual decision-making in relation to the prevention of drug abuse, cancer, and HIV/AIDS infection.

At Indiana University's 1997 Founder's Day Celebration, Torabi received the prestigious George Pinnell Outstanding Service Award and was named Chancellor's Professor, a title that honors faculty members who have achieved local, national, and international distinction in both teaching and research. Torabi was the first (and to date the only) such named professor in the school's history.

Among Dean Torabi's many awards and honors are the Alliance Scholar Award from the American Alliance for Health,

Physical Education, Recreation, and Dance (AAHPERD); the Distinguished Scholar Award from the International Council for Health, Physical Education, Recreation, Sport, and Dance; the Professional Service to Health Education Award from the American Association for Health Education; a Scholar Award from the American Association for Health Education; the American School Health Research Council Award; the Wild and White Scholar Award from the University of Northern Iowa; the Charles C. Cowell Lecturership and the Distinguished Alumni Award from Purdue University; and the Tony and Mary Hullman Health Achievement Award, presented by the Indiana Public Health Foundation. In 2002, Torabi was the recipient of the William A. Howe Award, the American School Health Association's highest honor, in recognition of outstanding contributions and distinguished service in school health. He presented the 2001 Scholar of the Year address during the National Conference of the American Association for Health Education and made the keynote presentation at the inaugural meeting of the American Academy of Health Behavior.

Dean Torabi is a Fellow of the American Academy of Health Behavior; Fellow and Charter Member of the North American Society for Health, Physical Education, Recreation, and Sport Professionals; Fellow of the American School Health Association; and Fellow of the American Association for Health Education. In 1996, the School of HPER recognized Dean Torabi with its Outstanding Researcher Award. Dean Torabi served as President of the American Academy of Health Behavior in 2004. Eta Sigma Gamma presented him with the 2003 Honor Award, the highest recognition bestowed for leadership in the health education profession.

While Torabi served as Interim Dean, he led the School of HPER through its transition to becoming one of Indiana University's two new schools of public health.

Mohammad Torabi. Courtesy of IU School of Public Health–Bloomington.

In preparation for the sixtieth anniversary of the school, Dean David Gallahue commissioned interviews of retired faculty members to be published and distributed during the April 2007 celebration. Gallahue was often heard remarking that the faculty of the school had the privilege of "standing on the shoulders of those who preceded them." A great many of the school's faculty members achieved significant accomplishments and brought renown to Indiana University; so many, in fact, that it would be impossible to recognize them all within the confines of the present publication. We present here an illustrative selection of retired faculty members across the school's history who honored the school with their outstanding leadership and achievements. We hasten to note that this is only a sampling from the school's prominent faculty, and we urge interested readers to see the entire listing of emeritus faculty accomplishments that is held in the repository at the IU Archives. The remarkable accomplishments of current faculty continue to bring academic recognition and professional acclaim to the school. Interested readers are encouraged to visit the new School of Public Health–Bloomington website for more information about recent faculty achievements.

GEORGE E. SCHLAFER, Assistant Professor Emeritus of Recreation (1916–1950)

George Schlafer's long association with Indiana University began in 1916, when he joined the faculty of the University Extension Division. In addition to his primary responsibility of teaching extension courses on play and recreation, he organized the first state conference on recreation and directed the first all-campus recreation program, which was the forerunner to the campus intramural program. His work with the university was interrupted by his service during World War I. In 1919, he returned to the campus as a member of the Department of Physical Education, where he organized and directed intramural activities for the next twenty-five years. He developed the first recreation course, The Nature and Practice of Play. The course was affectionately called Bean Bag by his students.

Schlafer served as the first Chair of the Recreation Department at the founding of the School of HPER. He coauthored *Physical Fitness for Boys: A Manual for the Instructor of the Service Program*, authored *Joy and Health through Play*, and edited the first state bulletin on physical education. At the end of the 1947–1948 academic year, after thirty years of pioneering work at Indiana University, Schlafer stepped down as chair of the department and returned to full-time teaching.

JANE FOX, Associate Professor Emeritus of Physical Education for Women (1927–1965)

(See faculty photograph on page 86.)
Jane Fox was recognized as an early innovator in folk, natural, and modern dance. According to Fox, this form of dance honored the work of the great Isadora Duncan. A hallmark of natural dance is the expression of feelings and ideas through movements more natural than the technical steps of traditional dance forms such as ballet. Modern dance of today has its roots in natural dance. Fox worked tirelessly to bring dance forward as a form of art and as a discipline, which by 1949 had eventuated in the formation of the dance major in the school.

EDNA MUNRO, Professor Emeritus of Physical Education for Women (1928–1961)

The appointment of Edna Munro was accompanied by the beginning of the Great Depression. Thus, it was at a time of financial stress that greatly challenged the growth of the Department of Physical Education for Women. Munro demonstrated abundant initiative and creativity in accomplishing the needs of a growing program, department, and facilities during the Depression Era. When she was appointed, there were only five full-time faculty members in the department and one part-time graduate

Edna Munro, 1941. Photograph from the 1941 Arbutus yearbook, page 232. Photograph by IU Photographic Services. Courtesy of IU Archives (P0034931).

George Schlafer, March 1942. He was Head of Intramurals at the time and the first Chair of the Department of Recreation. Photograph from the 1942 Arbutus yearbook, page 262. Photograph by IU Photographic Services. Courtesy of IU Archives (P0037250).

Karl Bookwalter, August 13, 1948. Photograph by IU Photographic Services. Courtesy of IU Archives (P0026754).

assistant; by 1958–1959, replacements and appointments of additional members had resulted in a total of ten faculty members. Munro's leadership during this period reflected wisdom and strong guidance. There were changes not only in curriculum but also in attire. One of the most interesting transformations came when women quit wearing bloomers for class activities. First, the long black stockings were traded for white anklets; then, the full black bloomers yielded to the less full black knickers. From knickers, the uniform evolved to a one-piece cotton suit and finally to the familiar shorts and blouse uniform.

KARL BOOKWALTER, Professor Emeritus of Physical Education for Men (1930–1969)

Karl Bookwalter initially joined Indiana University as an instructor in the School of Education. In 1946, he became Associate Professor of Physical Education and Director of the Bureau of Service and Research in the new School of HPER. In 1951–1952, Bookwalter completed an eight-week survey of Army Camps for the US Army and served as a consultant during that period, rendering 221 consultant services in physical education to 25 states and 25 foreign countries.

During the period of 1962–1965, Bookwalter was appointed to the additional office of Chair of the Graduate Division in the school. Among his many accomplishments, Bookwalter served two years as Chair of the National Committee on Facilities for Physical Education, which resulted in two significant publications, *College Facilities for Physical Education, Health Education, and Recreation* and *A Guide for Planning Facilities for Athletics, Recreation, Physical and Health Education*. He also served as Chair of the Research Section of the American Association for Health, Physical Education, and Recreation. In honor of his service as Chair of the Leader's Training Committee of the Boy Scouts of America, he was bestowed their highest honor—the Silver Beaver Award.

MARJORIE PHILLIPS, Professor (1941–1961, died while in service to IU)

(See faculty photograph on page 86.)

Marjorie Phillips was the first faculty member in the Department of Physical Education for Women to hold a doctorate. She was considered to be an outstanding teacher and was much loved by students. Her professional interests and contributions centered in the areas of tests, measurements, and research. Phillips was inducted into the American Academy of Physical Education in 1957, joining five other members of the school faculty, and was also named a Fellow in the American Association for Health, Physical Education, and Recreation. In 1961, she was awarded Indiana University's prestigious Frederic Bachman Lieber Award for Distinguished Teaching. When the death of this much-beloved teacher on July 9, 1961, was reported to the Board of Trustees, the board adopted a resolution in recognition of Marjorie Phillips for outstanding teaching and research.

GARRETT EPPLEY, Professor Emeritus of Recreation (1946–1967)

In 1946, Garrett G. Eppley was appointed Associate Professor of Recreation Education and Consultant in Recreation for State Parks, Cities, and Schools. Eppley was appointed as Acting Chair in 1947, replacing George Schlafer. He became Chair in 1953. He was widely recognized for his many professional contributions. He was President of the College Recreation Association, the Federation of National Professional Organizations for Recreation, and the American Institute of Park Executives. A pivotal contribution was his involvement in the merging of diverse park and recreation organizations into the NRPA. In the state of Indiana, he led the development of the Indiana Park and Recreation Association, founded the Great Lakes Park Training Institute, served as President of the Governor's Advisory Committee on

Garrett Eppley, December 1948. Photograph by IU Photographic Services. Courtesy of IU Archives (P0053037).

Recreation, and authored the Indiana Park and Recreation Law and its revision. He coauthored *A Guide for Community Recreation*, published by the Indiana State Board of Health. He was honored for his commitment to the concerns of Indiana's elderly as Older Hoosier of the Year in 1978.

REYNOLD CARLSON, Professor Emeritus of Recreation (1947–1972)

Reynold Carlson, formerly with the National Recreation Association, was first appointed Assistant Professor of Recreation and, in 1962, became Chair of the Department of Recreation. Carlson was recognized as an outstanding leader in outdoor recreation/education, conservation, and organized camping. He was also a master teacher who influenced many students in deep and lasting ways. He provided instrumental leadership in the development of the outdoor recreation education curriculum, as well as the Bradford Woods Outdoor Education and Camping Center. In 1949, he taught the first course at Bradford Woods and conducted the first Outdoor Recreation Workshop. He was highly influential in the establishment of Camp Riley and the American Camping Association Headquarters at Bradford Woods.

In 1956–1957, Carlson was appointed to President Eisenhower's Advisory Committee on Youth Fitness. He received a Fellow Award from the Association of Interpretive Naturalists and the American Camping Association's highest tribute, the Distinguished Service Award. Professor Carlson was a Founding

Fellow of the Academy of Leisure Sciences. In recognition of his outstanding contributions, he was awarded a Doctor of Humane Letters by Indiana University at the Bloomington Commencement on May 7, 1983. He also received an honorary Doctor of Humane Letters from Springfield College (1967).

Reynold Carlson. Courtesy of IU Archives (P005310).

(facing) Women's Physical Education faculty, 1944.
Front row (seated), from left to right: Eloise Ridder, Jane Fox, Helen Yeakel.
Back row (standing), from left to right: Marjorie Phillips, Naomi Leyhe,
unknown individual. Photograph from the 1944 Arbutus yearbook, page 183.
Photograph by IU Photographic Services. Courtesy of IU Archives (P0026841).

Jesse Keogh Rash, February 28, 1962. Photograph by IU Photographic Services. Courtesy of IU Archives (P0053030).

JESSE KEOGH RASH, Professor Emeritus of Health and Safety Education (1949–1976)

J. Keogh Rash was first appointed as Assistant Professor and in 1952, he succeeded Wesley Dane as second Chair of the Department of Health and Safety. Rash was a staunch supporter of the philosophy of health and safety education as an autonomous discipline, and he pioneered curriculum development in this area. His accomplishments encompassed a rich and varied record of research, publication, and public and professional service. He authored numerous articles, monographs, and books, including *The Health Education Curriculum*. Rash served as President of the American School Health Association and received outstanding service awards from Phi Delta Kappa; the American School Health Association; the Indiana Public Health Association; and the Indiana Association for Health, Physical Education, and Recreation. In 1974 he received the first Honor Award from Eta Sigma Gamma. He was a Fellow of the American School Health Association, American Public Health Association, and the American Academy of Political and Social Science. Rash received the Howe Award in 1969, the highest honor bestowed by the American School Health Association. In 1970–1971, he served as President of the Monroe County Public Health Nursing Association Board; was a member of the State Board of Health Advisory Committee on Drug Education; and was Chair of the Committee on Professional Education and Certification of Health Educators for the School Health Section of the American Public Health Association.

JANET R. MACLEAN, Professor Emeritus of Recreation (1951–1982)

Janet R. MacLean was first appointed as Instructor in Recreation and Campus Recreation Consultant in 1951. Dr. MacLean was well-known both nationally and internationally as a pioneer for the park and recreation movement, as well as for the concerns of the aging and aged. With the founding of the IU Center on Aging and the Aged in 1979, she was appointed as the center's first director and also awarded the title of Byron A. Root Professor in Aging.

Dr. MacLean was at the forefront of leading the NRPA in the development of the National Council on Accreditation, for which she served as Chair. She also served as Vice President of Recreation for both the state and district units of the American Association for Health, Physical Education, Recreation, and Dance. She wrote the initial bylaws for the Society of Park and Recreation Educators, for which she also served as President. She was a member of the NRPA Board of Trustees, as well. She founded the Western Access Video Excellence (WAVE) Award program for audio-visual excellence. Dr. MacLean served for five years on the President's Council on Fitness and Sports, and she served as delegate and featured speaker at three White House Conferences on Aging.

MacLean received many awards and honors for her accomplishments, including the coveted Silver Anniversary Award from the President's Council on Physical Fitness and Sports, a Sagamore of the Wabash, the Distinguished Service Award from the Society of Park and Recreation Educators, the NRPA Special Service Citation, Outstanding Educator of America, and the prestigious Senator Richard Lugar Vitae Bonae Award. She received the coveted Rocking Chair Award from Sigma Delta Chi Society of Professional Journalists at Indiana University, which honors a retiring faculty or staff member whose career has been notably distinguished. MacLean also was selected as a J. B. Nash

Janet MacLean, March 26, 1963. Photograph by IU News Bureau. Courtesy of IU Archives (P0050073).

Scholar-Lecturer. She was an elected Fellow of the Academy of Leisure Sciences and was a founding Fellow of the Academy for Parks and Recreation Administration.

*Donald J. Ludwig, November 2, 1959. Photograph by IU Photographic Services.
Courtesy of IU Archives (P0053031).*

DONALD J. LUDWIG, Professor Emeritus of Health and Safety Education (1952–1984)

Donald Ludwig served as Acting Chair of the Department of Health and Safety in 1956–1957 and began his term as Chair in 1972, serving nine years in this capacity. During his academic career, Professor Ludwig was consultant to and evaluator of academic programs in health and safety at Michigan State, North Carolina State, Tennessee, Louisiana State, and Florida State Universities. He was Consultant for the American Medical Association's Eleventh National Conference on Physicians and Schools. In 1977, the American Medical Association presented him with the School Bell Award for his six consecutive years of service as a consultant. Professor Ludwig received an outstanding teaching award at the 1968 Founder's Day and received the Indiana Association for Health Leadership award. He also was the recipient of the Amoco Foundation Award in 1969, which was a university-wide teaching award at the time. In 1980, he received a Citation of Honor from Eta Sigma Gamma in recognition of his role as an esteemed teacher and national leader in health education. He received the Leadership Award from the Indiana Association for Health, Physical Education, and Recreation, was a Fellow in the American School Health Association, and received a Service Key from Alpha Chapter of Phi Delta Kappa.

THEODORE DEPPE, Professor Emeritus of Recreation (1953–1987)

Ted Deppe served as Acting Chair of the school's Graduate Division and Acting Chair of the Bureau of Service and Research in 1965. In 1966, he was appointed Chair of the Department of Recreation and Park Administration, a position he held until his retirement in 1986. Under Deppe's leadership, Indiana University's program in Recreation and Park Administration gained national prominence.

During his career, Professor Deppe served in many professional leadership roles, including as President of the College Recreation Association, of the Society of Park and Recreation Educators, and of the Indiana Park and Recreation Association. He also was elected to the Board of Governors for the NRPA. Deppe received the Outstanding Service Award from the Indiana Park and Recreation Association. He was instrumental in developing Indiana University's Executive Development Program for park and recreation administrators and was a founding editor for the *Journal of Park and Recreation Administration*. In 1980, Ted Deppe was selected as a Founding Fellow of the Academy of Leisure Sciences, followed by his service as a Founding Fellow of the Academy for Parks and Recreation Administration.

Theodore Deppe. Photograph by IU Photographic Services. Courtesy of IU Archives (P0053041).

Bernard Loft, July 10, 1962. Photograph by IU Photographic Services. Courtesy of IU Archives (P0031138).

BERNARD I. LOFT, Professor Emeritus of Health and Safety Education (1956–1980)

Bernard Loft was the driving force behind the establishment of the Center for Safety and Traffic Education (later renamed the Center for Health and Safety Studies). He was the recipient of numerous honors and awards throughout his career. He served as an educational consultant for the American Automobile Association and was invited by President Lyndon Johnson to participate in the White House Conference on Health in November 1965. He was a Fellow of the American Academy of Safety Education and received the Distinguished Alumni Award from West Chester State College. He also participated in White House Conferences on Health and Occupational Safety.

JAMES E. "DOC" COUNSILMAN, Professor Emeritus of Kinesiology (1957–1990)

In 1957, James "Doc" Counsilman moved his family to Bloomington, Indiana, to take up his appointment as Assistant Swimming Coach and Assistant Professor of Physical Education for Men. He was promoted to Head Swimming Coach the next year. Doc Counsilman was both a highly successful coach and a prolific academic. By 1960, he was urging the trustees to build an outdoor swimming pool, which would ultimately serve as a training facility for his competitive swimmers. By 1964, Doc was serving as Head Coach of the US Olympic Swimming Team and as President of both the Swimming Hall of Fame and the American Swimming Coaches Administration. In 1966–1967, Counsilman served as Chair of the Olympic Swimming Development Committee, President of the Swimming Hall of Fame, and the Directing Coach of both the Italian and Mexican Olympic swimming teams. These roles were in addition to his coaching and teaching responsibilities at Indiana University. He authored a major book, *The Science of Swimming*, which went through five printings, three other books, and more than one hundred articles. In 1972, Counsilman produced four training films, *The Science of Swimming*, which were distributed worldwide.

Doc Counsilman's IU swimmers won twenty consecutive Big Ten Championships, from 1961 to 1981. He was named National Swimming Coach of the Year in 1969 and 1971 and was awarded the Certificate of Merit by the International Swimming Foundation. Counsilman was inducted into the International Swimming and Diving Hall of Fame in 1976. He swam the English Channel at age fifty-eight, becoming the oldest man at that time to successfully complete the swim.

In 1984–1985, Counsilman served as President of the Swimming Hall of Fame and was a member of the American Swimming Coaches Board of Directors, the American Olympic Committee Board of Directors, the New Zealand Olympic Committee, and the Mexican Olympic Committee. As reported at the meeting of the Board of Trustees in June 1989, Doc Counsilman was honored in Florida with the Gold Medallion from the International Swimming Hall of Fame. The James E. "Doc" Counsilman Aquatic Center in the Student Recreational Sports Center opened its doors in the summer of 1995.

"Doc" Counsilman and Chester Jastremski, swimming team, February 19, 1962. Photograph by the Athletic Department and John McGinnis. Courtesy of IU Archives (P0022984).

Evelyn Davies. Courtesy of IU School of Public Health–Bloomington.

EVELYN DAVIES, Professor Emeritus of Physical Education (1958–1981)

Evelyn Davies was an expert in adapted physical education, as well as a certified physical therapist. In 1970–1971, Davies received the first grant for curriculum development and graduate student support in adapted physical education from the US Department of Health, Education and Welfare. In 1972–1973, she received a grant for graduate degree preparation in physical education for the handicapped, which was renewed in 1973–1974. In 1978–1979, Davies received a Bureau for the Education of the Handicapped grant to support predoctoral professional preparation in adapted physical education. She was one of the most prolific externally funded researchers in the school during her career. Davies is credited for completing ground-breaking professional preparation and curriculum development in the area of adapted physical education.

JOHN M. COOPER, Professor Emeritus of Physical Education (1966–1982)

John Cooper was appointed as Professor of Physical Education for Men and Director of Graduate Studies in the school in 1966. In 1968, he was given the additional title of Associate Dean. Cooper was a renowned pioneer in the field of biomechanics and human movement; he was often referred to as the father of the jump shot in basketball. As a part of Cooper's interest in studying elite athlete performance, he sought research opportunities in athletic competitions. In 1978 the US Olympic Committee established the first National Sports Festival, which later was called the US Olympic Festival. Using high-speed film cameras to record the performances of some of America's best athletes in the long jump, triple jump, and hurdle, Cooper produced detailed descriptions of the velocities, joint angles, and other movement data, which was used by scientists and coaches to improve Olympic athletes' performance. This work inspired the beginning of the USOC's High Performance Division.

Among Cooper's many accomplishments was his leadership as President of the National Foundation of the American Association for Health, Physical Education, and Recreation (AAHPER); and President of the AAHPER. He received a Citation for Professional Service from the University of Toledo. Noted for his unique and pioneering work in the field of kinesiology, the National Academy of Kinesiology sponsored a national lectureship in his name. Cooper was awarded the Hetherington Award by the National Academy in 1994, and, the following year, he was bestowed the Luther Halsey Gulick Award, the highest honor given in the field of kinesiology.

The IU Board of Trustees approved the renaming of the graduate program in the Department of Kinesiology as the John M. Cooper Kinesiology Program in his honor. Cooper literally changed the way kinesiology is taught in the United States.

JAMES W. CROWE, Professor Emeritus of Applied Health Science (1966–2000)

James Crowe was recruited to Indiana University in 1966 to teach in the area of health education and to expand the area of safety education. His early efforts included the expansion of the department's driver education certification program, which eventually led to the certification of over 150 driver education teachers per year. In following years, his work led to the expansion of the department's offerings in the area of first aid and emergency care, which eventually expanded to include Emergency Medical Technician certification. In 1993, he assumed the

John Cooper, November 2, 1966. Photograph by IU Photographic Services. Courtesy of IU Archives (P0053039).

James W. Crowe, June 7, 1983. Photograph by IU Photographic Services. Courtesy of IU Archives (P0053075).

James A. Peterson, May 29, 1973. Photograph by IU Photographic Services. Courtesy of IU Archives (P0053033).

Chair of the Department of Applied Health Science and became Director of the Center for Health and Safety Studies.

Crowe served as President of the School and Community Safety Society of America in 1994–1995. Dr. Crowe was awarded the Amoco Outstanding Teaching Award from Indiana University in 1997. In 1996, he received the Distinguished Scholar

Award from the School and Community Safety Society of America, and the next year, he received the C. P. Youst Distinguished Service Award from the same organization. Crowe served as the college representative to the State Department of Public Instruction, Driver Education Curriculum Advisory Committee, and as Chair of the University Drug Commission.

JAMES A. PETERSON, Professor Emeritus of Recreation
and Park Administration (1967–1990)

James Peterson was appointed as Specialist in Recreation and
Parks for the state of Indiana in 1967 in conjunction with a joint
appointment between the Department of Recreation and Park
Administration at IU and the Cooperative Extension Service
at Purdue. His responsibilities included serving as a recreation
specialist to work with the people of Indiana through the state's
ninety-two county extension offices. Peterson's many leadership positions included serving on the Board of Directors for
the NRPA, and in 1987 he was elected President of NRPA. He
received the Meritorious Service Award and the Distinguished
Professional Award from NRPA. He was also the recipient of an
Award of Merit from the American Park and Recreation Society
and a Man of the Year Award from the Indiana Park and Recreation Association.

Peterson was a Founding Fellow of the Academy for Parks
and Recreation Administration. Hanover College recognized
Peterson with its Alumni Achievement Award for meritorious
service to the profession. Throughout his career, Peterson was
the consummate leader/servant in the recreation and park
profession. His joint appointment between IU and Purdue
provided the unusual opportunity to bring the resources of
these two universities together on important problems in the
park and recreation field in the state of Indiana, as well as
throughout the nation.

CLINTON STRONG, Professor Emeritus of Kinesiology (1969–1992)

Clinton Strong was heavily involved in the activities of the
Education Committee of the USOC throughout the 1970s and
1980s. He was particularly active in organizing special educational symposiums and Olympic Academies held at various sites
throughout the United States and in Olympia, Greece. He served

Clinton Strong, June 1984. Photograph by IU News Bureau.
Courtesy of IU Archives (P0053128).

as Director and Coordinator of two of the most successful
academies, one of which was held in Bloomington in 1980 and
the other in Indianapolis in 1987.

In 1978, he became the coordinator of continuing education
and off-campus programs for the School of HPER. In this
capacity he served for fourteen years as the liaison between

the School of HPER in Bloomington and the School of Physical Education at IUPUI, coordinating the many graduate courses offered by Bloomington faculty on the IUPUI campus. Strong played a unique role in the preparation of large numbers of graduate students. Unlike most courses in the school, Strong's research methods class was required of almost all students, irrespective of departmental affiliation or major. Nearly 3,000 students enrolled in the course during his tenure, which he taught 112 times. He was especially loved by his students for his abundant enthusiasm for teaching. Strong received several honors and awards, including the Excellence Award and the Maurice O. Graff Distinguished Alumni Award, both from the University of Wisconsin–La Crosse. He was elected President of Phi Epsilon Kappa in 1987, the national professional physical education fraternity.

FRAN SNYGG, Professor of Kinesiology (1971–1996, died while in service to IU)

Fran Snygg was a consummate teacher of modern dance, dance theory and composition, and other arts-related courses. Several of her students went on to work with major New York dance companies. She also taught modern dance to children in collaboration with IU's Ballet Department. Snygg was instrumental in organizing the annual Arts Week, which was and continues to be a collaboration between IU and the Bloomington community. She had a boundless spirit and was fully devoted to the mission of Arts Week.

While in service to IU, Fran Snygg held multiple appointments, including Professor of Kinesiology, Associate Dean of the Faculties, Professor of Theatre and Drama, and part-time Associate Professor of Music. She was a highly appreciated teacher and campus leader. At the age of fifty-four, Snygg died while in service to Indiana University.

Fran Snygg, August 7, 1984. Photograph by IU Photographic Services. Courtesy of IU Archives (P0053046).

An *Indiana Daily Student* article from February 18, 2010, provides a brief glimpse into her character:

> Fran Snygg had a laugh that rippled through every corridor she walked down. It was childlike, the kind of uproariously whimsical sound that would inspire laughter from others. The outgoing New York dancer, choreographer and artist never met a stranger.

She was deeply loved by her students and colleagues, and continues to this day to be missed as an ever positive presence on the Bloomington campus.

RICHARD F. MULL, Director of Recreational Sports (1972–2007)

Rich Mull was appointed as Director of Intramural Sports for Men and Assistant Professor of Physical Education for Men in the school in 1972. His title was changed to Director of Recreational Sports in 1976. Rich was instrumental in advancing campus recreation to divisional status, and during his leadership as Director, he also managed the Outdoor Pool and the IU Tennis Pavilion. He taught courses on recreational sport management in the Department of Recreation and Park Administration and is coauthor of *Recreational Sport Management*, a major textbook in the field. His service as Special Assistant to the Dean was instrumental at the time that the new recreational sports facility was designed and built. After the Student Recreational Sports Center was completed in 1995, his new responsibilities included: Special Assistant to the Dean, Director of the Tennis Pavilion and the Outdoor Pool, and Adjunct Professor in the Department of Recreation and Park Administration. Rich is considered to be a pioneer and national leader in the recreational sports field. He served as Executive Vice-President of the National Intramural Association and has received many recognitions and honors during his career. Among his many awards are the Honor Award

Richard Mull, September 20, 1994. Photograph by IU Photographic Services. Courtesy of IU Archives (P0053108).

from the National Intramural-Recreational Sports Association in 1985–1986 and the Office of Women's Affairs Athletic Award in 2006.

Ruth Engs, December 5, 1990. Photograph by IU News Bureau. Courtesy of IU Archives (P0053079).

RUTH ENGS, Professor Emeritus of Applied Health Science (1973–2003)

Ruth Engs, well-known expert on the topic of addiction, gave the country vital information about alcohol consumption from her national Student Alcohol Questionnaire, which was conducted from 1974 to 1994. Beyond her inquiry into alcohol consumption, she investigated tobacco, marijuana, and caffeine use; the influence of information on warning labels on addictive behavior; women's health issues; and the clean living movement. Engs' work revealed that the nation regularly goes through cycles of what she called a "clean living movement wherein alcohol, tobacco, and other substances are frowned upon." These periods are heavy with moral overtones, as well as with a sense of urgency and finality. Engs, frequently sought after to appear in national forums ranging from broadcast news to printed news media, was honored for her leadership and research as the recipient of the Robert H. Kirk Distinguished Doctoral Alumni Award in Health and Safety from the University of Tennessee in 1997. She also received the Distinguished HPER Researcher Award. Ruth Engs served as Chair of the National Association for Sport and Physical Education Sports Arts Academy in 1994–1995. Her research has appeared in prestigious publications including the *Congressional Quarterly*, the *Washington Post*, and leading public health and psychiatric journals. As of this writing, she has made over 300 research and other presentations and has published over 150 articles and 11 books.

DAVID R. AUSTIN, Professor Emeritus of Recreation and Park Administration (1976–2005)

David Austin's leadership in the profession was exemplary, as documented by his lengthy record of scholarly and professional activities. He published more than 150 journal articles, as well as numerous abstracts and book chapters, and authored or coauthored four highly influential textbooks in the field of therapeutic recreation. Austin received the National Literary Award from the NRPA and was inducted as Fellow in the prestigious Academy of Leisure Sciences. Austin served as President of both the American Therapeutic Recreation Association and the Academy of Leisure Sciences. He received the Distinguished Fellow Award from three organizations: the American Therapeutic Recreation Association, the National Therapeutic Recreation Society, and the Society of Park and Recreation Educators (SPRE). He also received a Teaching Excellence Award from SPRE.

Austin received the Brightbill Award from the University of Illinois, and the NRPA WAVE Award for Best Film, Camping and Recreational Programs for the Handicapped. He said his most meaningful honor was the Frederic Bachman Lieber Memorial Award, IU's oldest and most prestigious teaching award, which he received in 1988. Austin was named the J. B. Nash Scholar by the American Association for Leisure and Recreation. During his career, Austin was awarded several large federal grants to support the development of professional preparation in the field of recreation therapy. The Recreation Therapy Video Project (1993–1997) produced under his direction twenty-three instructional videos on various topics related to therapeutic recreation.

MARY LOU REMLEY, Professor Emeritus of Kinesiology (1976–1996)

Mary Lou Remley came to Indiana University in 1976, and in addition to her teaching appointment in the school, she also served as Adjunct Professor of Women's Studies in the College of Arts and Sciences and briefly, in 1986, as Acting Dean for Women's Affairs. Remley was a leader in the field of sport history and a voice for faculty governance, academic freedom, and gender equality. She served as President of the Bloomington Faculty Council and Co-President of the University Faculty Council and

David R. Austin, October 19, 1995. Photograph by IU Photographic Services. Courtesy of IU Archives (P0053071).

Mary Lou Remley, December 5, 1990. Photograph by IU News Bureau. Courtesy of IU Archives (P0053126).

Wynn Updyke, June 21, 1984. Photograph by IU Photographic Services. Courtesy of IU Archives (P0053130).

was a member of the Athletics Committee. Her service extended to the position of President of the North American Society for Sport History from 1981 to 1983 and of the National Association for Physical Education in Higher Education in 1991.

Remley was a recipient of the Alumni Merit Award from Southern Missouri State University and the Outstanding

Civilian Service Medal from the US Military Academy. In 1984, she was a Distinguished Lecturer in residence at Texas Women's University and a Visiting Scholar at the University of Georgia. Remley was honored as the featured presenter for the Amy Morris Homens Lecture at the AAHPERD National Convention in 1990.

WYNN UPDYKE, Professor Emeritus of Kinesiology (1977–1997)

Wynn Updyke was appointed as Professor of Physical Education and Associate Dean of Graduate Studies in 1977; later he was appointed Associate Dean for Academic Affairs and Research. Updyke's research contributions were in the study of fitness. He was Director of the Amateur Athletic Union (AAU) Physical Fitness Testing and Awards Program. In 1981–1982, the School of HPER became the administrative site for this AAU program. As Director of the AAU Fitness Projects and the President's Challenge Program, Updyke secured over twenty-five separate contracts totaling over $15 million. Under his leadership, the President's Challenge Program touched the lives of over sixty million youths. Updyke's pioneering research provided a fifteen-year data profile concerning fitness trends in children and youth ages six through seventeen.

Updyke received honors from various societies and organizations, including the Joy of Effort Award from the National Association for Sport and Physical Education, and the Distinguished Administrator Award and Dudley Allen Sargent Lecture Award from the National Association for Physical Education in Higher Education. In 1990, Updyke was inducted into the Roberts Wesleyan College Athletic Hall of Fame for his basketball achievements as a player and a coach. In 1991, he was one of ten individuals recognized with the Healthy American Fitness Leaders Award sponsored by the US Chamber of Commerce in conjunction with the National Fitness Leaders Association and the American Council on Exercise.

HAROLD H. MORRIS, Professor Emeritus of Kinesiology (1978–2003)

Hal Morris was appointed as Associate Professor of Physical Education in 1978 and in 1983 he assumed the position of Chair of the Department of Physical Education, a position he held until 2001. Morris' specialties were in the areas of motor

Harold H. Morris, May 20, 1986. Photograph by IU Photographic Services. Courtesy of IU Archives (P0053086).

control, reaction time as a function of sensory modality, and measurement and statistics. During his term as Chair, Morris devoted his considerable energy and talent to strengthening the department. He spearheaded a consensus-building process that resulted in 1989 in changing the name of the department to the Department of Kinesiology. The change in name signaled growth in the department's research stature, as well as the increasing importance of physical activity to achieving positive health outcomes in individuals of all ages and abilities.

Morris provided important leadership in major professional organizations, including as Chair of the Measurement and Evaluation Council, President of the Research Consortium, and President of the American Alliance for Health, Physical Education, Recreation, and Dance (AAHPERD). He also received an Honor Award from the AAHPERD. Morris was recognized as a Sagamore of the Wabash by the governor of Indiana. In recognition of his scholarship, he was elected as a Fellow of the American Academy of Kinesiology and Physical Education and received the Biannual Scholar Award from the International Council for Health, Physical Education, Recreation, Sport, and Dance. For his outstanding professional service, he received the 2002 Luther Halsey Gulick Medal, the highest award given by the AAHPERD. The award that Morris cherished the most was the School of HPER Outstanding Teacher Award, which he received in 2001.

GARY M. ROBB, Associate Professor (1979–2008)

Gary Robb was first appointed Director of Bradford Woods and Assistant Professor of Recreation and Park Administration, part-time, in 1979. The position of Director of the National Center on Accessibility was added in 1992. Under Gary Robb's leadership, Bradford Woods provided an outstanding residential experience in outdoor education for thousands of Indiana fifth graders. The school outdoor programs left an indelible imprint of love for the outdoors on the people of Indiana. He led in the development of a concept that could make all outdoor facilities accessible to persons with disabilities. Under Robb's leadership, the National Center on Accessibility increased access to the nation's national parks for all people. He received the Distinguished Service Award from the National Therapeutic Recreation Society in 1980 and served as a trustee of the NRPA in from

Gary M. Robb, September 21, 1982. Photograph by IU Photographic Services. Courtesy of IU Archives (P0053056).

1980 to 1982. He was named to President Reagan's National Committee on Employment of the Handicapped and received the 1985 Outstanding Alumni Award from the University of Utah, Department of Leisure and Recreation.

PAUL SURBURG, Professor Emeritus of Kinesiology (1979–2001)

Paul Surburg is recognized for developing and revising courses in adapted physical education and athletic training at both the undergraduate and graduate levels. His research interests were in motor learning and control, including such topics as the effects of mental imagery on motor skill acquisition, the effects of proprioceptive facilitation on movement initiation, and the effects of midline crossing inhibition on response processing. His dominant research pool comprised individuals from special populations, particularly those with mild mental retardation. His research was published in prestigious journals, including the *Adapted Physical Activity Journal*, the *Journal of Gerontology*, the *American Corrective Therapy Journal*, and the *American Journal of Mental Retardation*. He also contributed chapters to several publications. Surburg was a regular reviewer on grant review panels for the US Department of Education and was responsible for over $1 million in US Department of Education grants that supported eighty-five master's students and nineteen doctoral students in adapted physical education. His awards and honors include the G. L. Rarick Research Award for his research contributions dealing with special populations, the Teaching Excellence Recognition Award from Indiana University, and an Outstanding Teaching Award from the University of West Florida. The School of HPER had a long and distinguished history of leadership in the area of adapted physical education, and Surburg was considered one of the pioneers in this area, along with Arthur Daniels and Evelyn Davies.

Paul Surburg, December 15, 1990. Photograph by IU News Bureau. Courtesy of IU Archives (P0053087).

Ruth V. Russell, March 26, 1996. Photograph by IU Photographic Services. Courtesy of IU Archives (P0053084).

RUTH V. RUSSELL, Professor Emeritus of Recreation, Park, and Tourism Studies (1981–2010)

Ruth V. Russell's administrative skills were engaged by the school and the university through several appointments, including as Associate Dean for the school, Associate Dean of Faculties, and Associate Chair of the Department of Recreation, Park, and Tourism Studies. Further, she served as Director of the Leisure Research Institute, during which time she promoted faculty and student research. During her career, Russell was President of the SPRE and the founder of the Annual Teaching Institute. She served on the Board of Trustees for the NRPA. Her contributions have been widely recognized. She was elected Fellow of the Academy of Leisure Sciences and Fellow of the American Leisure Academy. She received the Distinguished Colleague Award and Outstanding Teaching Award from SPRE. She was the recipient of the Outstanding Teaching Award from the school and the Amoco Foundation Award for Distinguished Teaching at the university level. Her superior teaching skills contributed to her selection as a member of the IU Faculty Colloquium on Excellence in Teaching. Russell's courses were highly sought by students at all levels, from undergraduate through doctoral study. Russell published twelve books, many of which were leading textbooks in the field. During her career, she authored or coauthored over seventy publications.

JOEL F. MEIER, Professor Emeritus of Health, Physical Education, and Recreation (1994–2007)

Joel Meier was appointed as Professor of Recreation and Park Administration and Chair of the Department of Recreation and Park Administration in 1994. Prior to coming to Indiana University, Meier served as Associate Dean of the School of Forestry at the University of Montana. During his twenty-four years at Montana, he held various positions, including Chair of the

Department of HPER and Professor/Coordinator of Recreation Management in the School of Forestry.

Meier has influenced the direction and progress of the recreation and park profession in many ways. In whatever arena he worked, he quickly became a leader. He served as President of a number of professional organizations, including the American Alliance for Health, Physical Education, Recreation, and Dance; and the American Association for Leisure and Recreation. He served as Chair of the North American Society of Health, Physical Education, Recreation, and Dance, and he served on the AAHPERD Board of Governors for eight years. Meier was a Senior Fulbright Scholar in New Zealand, consultant to the Malaysian Ministry of Youth and Sport, and Distinguished Visiting Professor at the University of Alaska. Meier received the J. B. Nash Scholar Award from the American Association for Leisure and Recreation and the Luther Halsey Gulick Award, which is regarded as the highest honor of the AAHPERD in recognition of long and distinguished service to the organization. He also received the Julian Smith Award from the National Council on Outdoor Education and the Distinguished Colleague Award from the Society of Park and Recreation Educators for professional accomplishments and contributions to the profession. Meier's influence as a professor reached far and wide; many of his former students attained positions of leadership in the leisure services industry, as well as in higher education. In 2009 he received the prestigious Paul K. Petzoldt Award from the Wilderness Education Association, and in 2014 the IU Foundation honored Meier and his wife, Patti, with the Partners in Philanthropy Cornerstone Award in recognition of their exceptional leadership.

Also with Patti, Meier founded the Joel and Patricia Meier Outdoor Leadership Chair in the Department of Recreation and Park Administration beginning August 1998. Throughout the years and into the present, the Meiers have been exceptional leaders in supporting and promoting the school.

Joel F. Meier, September 7, 1999. Photograph by IU Photographic Services. Courtesy of IU Archives (P0053109).

Lloyd Kolbe. Photograph by Ann Erdenberger. Courtesy of Lloyd Kolbe.

LLOYD KOLBE, Professor Emeritus of Applied Health Science
(2003–2010)

Lloyd Kolbe was appointed as Professor of Applied Health Science in August 2003 and assumed the additional role of Associate Dean of Global and Community Health in 2009. He was Founding Director of the Division of Adolescent School Health in the National Center for Chronic Disease Prevention and Health Promotion of the CDCP. Kolbe's expertise is in obesity and related public health policy issues. He noted that obesity was both a serious health problem for the nation and an economic problem for the medical system and insurance companies.

In 2003–2004, Kolbe received the Award for Excellence in the Prevention and Control of Chronic Disease from the US Chronic Disease Directors for advancing knowledge and practice in reducing chronic disease burden. He was appointed by the National Academies' Institute of Medicine (IOM) to serve as Vice Chair of the IOM's Committee on Adolescent Health and Development. In 2007–2008, Kolbe was appointed as Chair of the Board of Scientific Counselors for the Coordinating Center for Health Promotion, CDCP. The fifteen-member board of top scientists provided advice to the Secretary of the US Department of Health and Human Services and to the CDCP Director. In 2000, he was awarded an Honorary Doctor of Humane Letters from Towson University.

JERRY DIANA WILKERSON, Professor Emeritus of Kinesiology (2003–2011)

Jerry Wilkerson was appointed Professor of Kinesiology and Executive Associate Dean of the school in 2003. Wilkerson had held numerous academic appointments prior to those at IU, most notably at Texas Woman's University as Chair of the Department of Kinesiology, the second-largest academic department at that institution. During her academic career, she advised more than thirty doctoral students, many of whom have attained the ranks of distinguished faculty, deans, and provosts at other universities. She wrote nearly fifty publications and participated in over seventy presentations, with concentrations in the areas of women in sport, physical therapy, independent living skills for older populations, MRI research, and adapted physical education. She was active in the Biomechanics Academy of the National Association for Sport and Physical Education and also served as Vice President of Publications of the International Biomechanics Society. As an administrator at Texas Women's University, she oversaw the construction of an 186,000-square-foot athletic/physical education facility that is a hallmark at the institution.

Among Wilkerson's many accomplishments at IU was the formation of the school's Anita Aldrich Distinguished Alumni Award, which recognizes those HPER alumni who have made significant contributions to the cause of women in sport and physical activity. The presentation of the award is a centerpiece of the annual National Girls and Women in Sport Day banquet, an event that Wilkerson helped organize. Wilkerson has received numerous honors and awards, including the Ruth B. Glasgow Award, given by the Biomechanics Academy Committee of the National Association for Sport and Physical Education. She was honored in 2013 as the recipient of the Anita Aldrich Distinguished Alumni Award.

Jerry Diana Wilkerson and Mohammad Torabi. Wilkerson receiving Aldrich Award, 2013. Courtesy of the School of Public Health–Bloomington.

Sarah Purpura, recipient of the Joan Weinberg Wolf Scholarship for Dietetics, School of Public Health–Bloomington Scholarship and Honors Dinner, September 20, 2013. Courtesy of IU School of Public Health–Bloomington.

Epilogue. Advancing the Legacy

When you put a cargo on board a ship, you make that venture on trust,
For you know not whether you will be drowned or come safe to land.
If you say, I will not embark till I am certain of my fate, *then you will do no trade.*—RUMI

THE ONGOING PURSUIT OF EFFECTIVE STRATEGIES FOR addressing the serious health problems of the nation has always been a central mission of the School of Health, Physical Education, and Recreation.

Throughout its history, the school has been home to some of the nation's best and most progressive programs in health, physical education, and recreation. As the needs of the country changed, so too did these programs, always staying at the forefront of research and service to the community. To respond to the challenges of the twenty-first century, the school would take on a new dimension, a new name, and broader horizons. As the IU School of Public Health–Bloomington, it is poised to meet the health and well-being needs of citizens, as well as the quality-of-life challenges in communities throughout the nation and the world. The new school will train professionals to address the real-world impact of unhealthy lifestyles, chronic disease, and threats to quality of life through education, prevention, and amelioration.

While the most pressing public health issues of the new century may be largely self-created through poor lifestyle choices, poor consumption patterns, environmental degradation, and increasingly high-stress employment conditions, modern medicine and containment practices alone cannot address these issues in isolation. Nor could traditional HPER professions, by

themselves, mend a nation at risk. To make a lasting contribution to this effort becomes the exciting challenge of the new School of Public Health.

The School of HPER bequeaths to the new school the knowledge, science, and professional skills that are its legacy so that IU School of Public Health–Bloomington may lead the nation in creating the social changes that will move prevention to the forefront of public health. Once again, Indiana University is positioned to lead the state, the nation, and partners around the world in the promotion of healthy lifestyles and healthier communities.

To evolve is not to throw away the past; rather, it is to embrace its legacy and transform it for a new generation. So too with the legacy of the IU School of Health, Physical Education, and Recreation and the new IU School of Public Health–Bloomington.

APPENDIX A. *Full-Time Faculty in Rank at Start of 2012–2013 Academic Year*

CHANCELLOR'S PROFESSOR

MOHAMMAD R. TORABI, MPH (Indiana University, 1984), PhD (Purdue University, 1982), MSPH (Tehran University, 1978), Chancellor's Professor in Applied Health Science and Interim Dean, School of Public Health–Bloomington

PROFESSORS

DONETTA J. COTHRAN, PhD (University of Maryland, 1996), Professor in Kinesiology

JESUS DAPENA, PhD (University of Iowa, 1979), Professor in Kinesiology

ALAN W. EWERT, PhD (University of Oregon, 1982), Professor in Recreation, Park, and Tourism Studies and the Patricia and Joel Meier Endowed Chair in Outdoor Leadership

LAWRENCE W. FIELDING, PhD (University of Maryland, 1974), Professor in Kinesiology

KATHLEEN R. GILBERT, PhD (Purdue University, 1987), Professor in Applied Health Science and Executive Associate Dean, School of Public Health–Bloomington

ROBERT M. GOODMAN, PhD (University of North Carolina, 1987), Professor in Applied Health Science

BARBARA A. HAWKINS, ReD (Indiana University, 1979), Professor in Recreation, Park, and Tourism Studies

LYNN JAMIESON, ReD (Indiana University, 1980), Professor in Recreation, Park, and Tourism Studies

JAMES E. KLAUNIG, PhD (University of Maryland, 1980), Professor in Environmental Health

DAVID M. KOCEJA, PhD (Indiana University, 1989), Professor and Chair in Kinesiology

DAVID LOHRMANN, PhD (University of Michigan, 1981), Professor and Interim Chair in Applied Health Science

LAURA A. MCCLOSKEY, PhD (University of Michigan, 1986), Professor in Applied Health Science

BRYAN P. MCCORMICK, PhD (Clemson University, 1993), Professor and Chair in Recreation, Park, and Tourism Studies and Interim Chair in Environmental Health

JOHN S. RAGLIN, PhD (University of Wisconsin, 1988), Professor in Kinesiology

CRAIG M. ROSS, ReD (Indiana University, 1980), Professor in Recreation, Park, and Tourism Studies

JOHN B. SHEA, PhD (University of Michigan, 1974), Professor in Kinesiology

JOEL M. STAGER, PhD (Indiana University, 1980), Professor in Kinesiology

JANET PATRICIA WALLACE, PhD (Pennsylvania State University, 1981), Professor in Kinesiology

WILLIAM L. YARBER, HSD (Indiana University, 1973), Professor in Applied Health Science; Professor of Gender Studies; Senior Director, Rural Center for AIDS/STD Prevention; Senior Research Fellow, The Kinsey Institute for Research in Sex, Gender, and Reproduction

CLINICAL PROFESSORS

CATHERINE A. GROVE, PhD (University of Missouri, 1990), Clinical Professor in Kinesiology; Athletic Trainer

JOHN W. SCHRADER, HSD, ATC (Indiana University, 1993), Clinical Professor and Associate Chair in Kinesiology

ASSOCIATE PROFESSORS

ROBERT E. BILLINGHAM, PhD (Virginia Polytechnic Institute and State University, 1979), Associate Professor in Applied Health Science

EARL BLAIR, EdD (University of Kentucky, 1997), Associate Professor in Applied Health Science

JOSEPH S. CHEN, PhD (Pennsylvania State University, 1996), Associate Professor in Recreation, Park, and Tourism Studies

SHU COLE, PhD (Texas A&M University, 1998), Associate Professor in Recreation, Park, and Tourism Studies

BRIAN DODGE, PhD (Indiana University, 2002), Associate Professor in Applied Health Science

NANCY T. ELLIS, HSD (Indiana University, 1979), Associate Professor in Applied Health Science

ALYCE D. FLY, PhD (University of Illinois, 1991), Associate Professor in Applied Health Science

GEORGIA C. FREY, PhD (Oregon State University, 1993), Associate Professor in Kinesiology

GWENDOLYN ANN HAMM, MS (Indiana University, 1972), Associate Professor in Kinesiology

BARBARA A. HOCEVAR, PhD (Case Western Reserve University, 1993), Associate Professor in Environmental Health

LISA M. KAMENDULIS, PhD (University of New Mexico, 1994), Associate Professor in Environmental Health

DOUGLAS H. KNAPP, PhD (Southern Illinois University, 1994), Associate Professor in Recreation, Park, and Tourism Studies

ALICE K. LINDEMAN, PhD (Syracuse University, 1986), Associate Professor in Applied Health Science

BETH E. MEYERSON, PhD (Saint Louis University, 2002), Associate Professor in Kinesiology

TIMOTHY MICKLEBOROUGH, PhD (Colorado State University, 2000), Associate Professor in Kinesiology

SUSAN E. MIDDLESTADT, PhD (University of California, 1979), Associate Professor in Applied Health Science

CECILIA SEM OBENG, PhD (Indiana University, 2002), Associate Professor in Applied Health Science

PAUL M. PEDERSEN, PhD (Florida State University, 2000), Associate Professor in Kinesiology

MICHAEL D. REECE, PhD (University of Georgia, 2000), Associate Professor and Director, Center for Sexual Health Promotion in Applied Health Science, and Associate Dean for Research and Graduate Studies, School of Public Health–Bloomington

GARY A. SAILES, PhD (University of Minnesota, 1984), Associate Professor in Kinesiology

DONG-CHUL SEO, PhD (Indiana University, 2004), Associate Professor in Applied Health Science

SUSAN M. SMITH, EdD (University of Tennessee, 1989), Associate Professor in Applied Health Science

CARRIE D. STEELE, PhD (University of Virginia, 2003), Associate Professor in Kinesiology

A. MARIEKE VAN PUYMBROECK, PhD (University of Florida, 2004), Associate Professor in Recreation, Park, and Tourism Studies

SARAH J. YOUNG, PhD (Indiana University, 1998), Associate Professor in Recreation, Park, and Tourism Studies

CLINICAL ASSOCIATE PROFESSORS

G. Keith Chapin, PhD (Michigan State University, 1995), Clinical Associate Professor in Kinesiology

Noy Kay, HSD (Indiana University, 1987), Clinical Associate Professor in Applied Health Science

Catherine M. Laughlin, HSD (Indiana University, 1998), Clinical Associate Professor and Associate Chair in Applied Health Science

Elizabeth L. Shea, MS (Pennsylvania State University, 1986), Clinical Associate Professor in Kinesiology

ASSISTANT PROFESSORS

Cem M. Basman, PhD (Colorado State University, 1998), Assistant Professor in Recreation, Park, and Tourism Studies

H. Charles Chancellor, PhD (Clemson University, 2005), Assistant Professor in Recreation, Park, and Tourism Studies

Robert F. Chapman, PhD (Indiana University, 1996), Assistant Professor in Kinesiology

Galen E. Clavio, PhD (Indiana University, 2008), Assistant Professor in Kinesiology

Jun Dai, PhD (Emory University, 2008), Assistant Professor in Applied Health Science

Shingairai A. Feresu, PhD (University of Michigan, 2001), Assistant Professor in Kinesiology

S. Lee Hong, PhD (Pennsylvania State University, 2007), Assistant Professor in Kinesiology

Jeanne Johnston, PhD (Indiana University, 2006), Assistant Professor in Kinesiology

Choong Hoon Lim, PhD (University of Maryland, 2007), Assistant Professor in Kinesiology

Hsien-Chang Lin, PhD (University of Michigan, 2010), Assistant Professor in Applied Health Science

Jonathan T. Macy, PhD (Indiana University, 2006), Assistant Professor Applied Health Science

N. Rasul Mowatt, PhD (University of Illinois, 2006), Assistant Professor in Recreation, Park, and Tourism Studies

Jennifer A. Piatt, PhD (University of Utah, 2007), Assistant Professor in Recreation, Park, and Tourism Studies

Barbara J. Van Der Pol, PhD (Indiana University, 2007) Assistant Professor in Kinesiology

Patrick T. Walsh, PhD (University of Minnesota, 2008), Assistant Professor in Kinesiology

Antonio Williams, PhD (Indiana University, 2010), Assistant Professor in Kinesiology

Wan-Teng A. Wong, MS (Indiana University, 2010), Assistant Professor in Applied Health Science

Ahmed H. Youssefagha, PhD (University of Louisville, 2006), Assistant Professor in Applied Health Science

CLINICAL ASSISTANT PROFESSORS

Charles D. Beeker, MS (Indiana University, 2003), Clinical Assistant Professor in Kinesiology and Director, Underwater Science Program

Phillip L. Henson, PhD (Indiana University, 1976), Clinical Assistant Professor in Kinesiology

Lesa Huber, PhD (University of Nebraska, 1989), Clinical Assistant Professor in Applied Health Science

Joanne C. Klossner, PhD (Indiana University, 2004), Clinical Assistant Professor in Kinesiology

Julia S. Knapp, PhD (Indiana University, 2000), Clinical Assistant Professor in Recreation, Park, and Tourism Studies

Maresa J. Murray, PhD (Michigan State University, 2001), Clinical Assistant Professor in Applied Health Science

Joanna M. Shimek, PhD (University of Illinois, 2010), Clinical Assistant Professor in Environmental Health

Kevin J. Slates, EdD (Spalding University, 2005), Clinical Assistant Professor in Applied Health Science

SENIOR LECTURERS AND CLINICAL SENIOR LECTURERS

Carol Armbruster-Kennedy, MS (Colorado State University, 1989), Senior Lecturer in Kinesiology

Lucinda Fox Cousins, MS (Northern Illinois University, 1973), Senior Lecturer in Kinesiology

Victoria M. Getty, MEd (Pennsylvania State University, 1987), Senior Lecturer in Applied Health Science

K. Michelle Miller, MS (Indiana University, 1996), Clinical Senior Lecturer in Kinesiology

William Ramos, MS (Indiana University, 1998), Senior Lecturer in Recreation, Park, and Tourism Studies

LECTURERS AND CLINICAL LECTURERS

TRENT APPLEGATE, HSD (Indiana University, 2003), Lecturer in Applied Health Science

HOLLY AUNGST, MA (Arizona State University, 2005), Lecturer in Kinesiology

KELLY J. BAUTE, MS (Indiana University, 2008), Lecturer in Kinesiology

LADONNA J. BLUEEYE, MPH (University of Oklahoma, 2003), Lecturer in Applied Health Science

SELENE CARTER, MFA (University of Wisconsin, 2005), Lecturer in Kinesiology

DEBORAH GETZ, ReD (Indiana University, 2000), Clinical Lecturer in Recreation, Park, and Tourism Studies and Director, Center for Student Leadership Development

MARGARET LION, MS (Indiana University, 1989), Lecturer in Kinesiology

ROBERT G. MORGAN, MA (Marshall University, 1973), Lecturer in Kinesiology

SHAHLA RAY, PhD (Hacettepe University, Ankara, Turkey, 1997), Lecturer in Applied Health Science

KRISHA THIAGARAJAH, PhD (Indiana University, 2005), Lecturer in Applied Health Science

RESEARCH SCIENTISTS

RUTH GASSMAN, PhD (Rutgers University, 1995), Associate Scientist and Director, Indiana Prevention Resource Center in Applied Health Science

DEBRA L. HERBENICK, PhD (Indiana University, 2007), Assistant Research Scientist in Applied Health Science

VANESSA R. SCHICK, PhD (George Washington University, 2009), Assistant Scientist in Applied Health Science

ACADEMIC SPECIALISTS

JOANNE BUNNAGE, PhD (Indiana University, 2003), Academic Specialist in Applied Health Science

ASGHAR GHARAKHANI, MS (Indiana University, 1975), Academic Specialist in Recreation, Park, and Tourism Studies

EVELYN S. GOLDSMITH, EdD (Indiana University of Pennsylvania, 1987), Academic Specialist in the School of Public Health–Bloomington

PATRICK KELLY, MS (Indiana University, 2006), Academic Specialist in Kinesiology

ROBERT G. KESSLER, MS (Indiana University, 1999), Academic Specialist and Curriculum and Physical Activity Coordinator in Kinesiology

CHARLES E. PEARCE, MS (Indiana University, 2004), Academic Specialist in Kinesiology

DAVID M. SKIRVIN, EdD (Indiana University, 1998), Academic Specialist and Assistant Dean in the School of Public Health–Bloomington

MICHAEL S. WILLETT, MS (Indiana University, 1987), Academic Specialist and Associate Chair in Kinesiology and Director, AAU Fitness Projects and President's Challenge

STEPHEN A. WOLTER, MS (Indiana University, 1980), Academic Specialist in Recreation, Park, and Tourism Studies and Director, Eppley Institute for Parks and Public Lands

SHERRIL L. YORK, PhD (Texas Woman's University, 1981), Academic Specialist in Recreation, Park and Tourism Studies and Director, National Center for Accessibility

DEANS

WILLARD W. PATTY, Professor Emeritus of Health and Safety, retired December 1957.

ARTHUR S. DANIELS, Professor of Physical Education, served as Dean until his death on June 18, 1966.

JOHN R. ENDWRIGHT, Professor Emeritus of Physical Education, retired December 1983.

ANITA ALDRICH, Professor Emeritus of Physical Education and of Education, retired May 1985.

TONY A. MOBLEY, Professor Emeritus of Recreation and Park Administration and Dean Emeritus of Health, Physical Education, and Recreation, retired June 2003.

DAVID L. GALLAHUE, Professor Emeritus of Kinesiology, retired June 2008.

DEPARTMENT OF APPLIED HEALTH SCIENCE

WILLIAM THOMAS BRENNAN, Associate Professor Emeritus of Health and Safety Education, retired June 1983.

JAMES W. CROWE, Professor Emeritus of Applied Health Science, retired September 2000.

C. WESLEY DANE, Assistant Professor Emeritus of Health and Safety Education, retired July 1973.

RUTH CLIFFORD ENGS, Professor Emeritus of Applied Health Science, retired May 2003.

BERNARD I. LOFT, Professor Emeritus of Health and Safety Education, retired July 1981.

DONALD L. LUDWIG, Professor Emeritus of Health and Safety Education, retired May 1984.

LLOYD KOLBE, Professor Emeritus of Applied Health Science, retired August 2010.

LOREN MITCHELL, Assistant Professor Emeritus, retired July 1972.

JESSE KEOGH RASH, Professor Emeritus of Health and Safety Education, retired July 1976.

NATHAN WILLIAM SHIER, Associate Professor Emeritus of Health and Safety, retired January 2008.

DALE WOMBLE, Professor Emeritus of Applied Health Science, retired May 1988.

Faculty members who retired after 2012 were retired from the new IU School of Public Health–Bloomington. The list includes retired faculty through to May 2014. It also includes faculty members who died while in service to the School of Health, Physical Education, and Recreation, Indiana University; these names are denoted with an asterisk (*).

DEPARTMENT OF KINESIOLOGY

ERNEST H. ANDRES, Assistant Professor Emeritus of Physical Education, retired January 1983.

JAMES J. BELISLE, Associate Professor Emeritus of Kinesiology, retired December 1996.

HOBART S. BILLINGSLEY, Associate Professor Emeritus of Kinesiology, retired December 1990.

KARL W. BOOKWALTER, Professor Emeritus of Physical Education for Men, retired September 1969.

JOHN P. BROGNEAUX, Assistant Professor Emeritus of Physical Education and of Education, retired July 1976.

*HOWARD K. BROWN, Instructor in Physical Education for Men, devoted his career service to Indiana University until the time of his death in 1975.

JAMES ROLLAR BROWN, Associate Professor Emeritus of Kinesiology, retired June 2003.

BENJAMIN F. BRUCE, Associate Professor Emeritus of Physical Education, retired August 1984.

CLUM C. BUCHER, Assistant Professor Emeritus of Physical Education for Men, retired July 1972.

DONALD J. BURNS, Associate Professor Emeritus, retired June 2006.

SANDRA KAY BURRUS, Associate Professor Emeritus of Kinesiology, retired December 2001.

RONALD PAUL CARLSON, Associate Professor Emeritus of Kinesiology, retired December 2000.

ZORA G. CLEVENGER, Professor Emeritus of Physical Education for Men, retired June 1947.

OWEN L. COCHRANE, Instructor in Physical Education for Men, retired August 1957.

JOHN M. COOPER, Professor Emeritus of Physical Education, retired June 1982.

JAMES COUNSILMAN, Professor Emeritus of Kinesiology, retired December 1990.

LUCINDA COUSINS, Senior Lecturer of Kinesiology, retired May 2013.

GEORGE F. COUSINS, Professor Emeritus of Physical Education, retired December 1985.

CHRIS DAL SASSO, Instructor in Physical Education for Men, retired December 1980.

JESUS DAPENA, Professor Emeritus of Kinesiology, retired May 2013.

JOHN B. DAUGHERTY, Professor Emeritus of Physical Education, retired December 1980.

EVELYN A. DAVIES, Professor Emeritus of Physical Education, retired December 1981.

LAWRENCE FIELDING, Professor Emeritus of Kinesiology, retired May 2014.

GORDON R. FISHER, Associate Professor Emeritus of Physical Education for Men, retired July 1962.

ROBERT FITCH, Assistant Professor of Physical Education, retired July 1989.

JANE FOX, Associate Professor Emeritus of Physical Education for Women, retired July 1965.

LEROY H. GETCHELL, Professor Emeritus of Kinesiology, retired December 1996.

GWENDOLYN HAMM, Associate Professor Emeritus of Kinesiology, retired May 2013.

*PAUL J. HARRELL, Associate Professor of Physical Education for Men, died in January 1973 while in service to Indiana University.

BETTY H. HAVEN, Clinical Associate Professor Emeritus of Kinesiology, retired August 2007.

PHILLIP HENSON, Clinical Assistant Professor Emeritus of Kinesiology, retired December 2013.

CLARA HESTER, Professor Emeritus of Physical Education (Normal College of the American Gymnastic Union, Indiana University), retired July 1968.

ROBERT BRUCE HICKS, Instructor Emeritus of Physical Education, retired December 1986.

SARAH MARGARET HOPE, Assistant Professor Emeritus of Physical Education, retired May 1987.

NORMA JEAN JOHNSON, Associate Professor Emeritus of Kinesiology, retired December 1996.

ROBERT E. LAWRENCE, Instructor of Kinesiology, retired August 2002.

NAOMI L. LEYHE, Professor Emeritus of Physical Education, retired May 1979.

LOLA LOHSE, Professor Emeritus of Physical Education, and Dean Emeritus, School of Physical Education, IUPUI, retired July 1977. (Professor Lohse was a member of the faculty of the Normal College when it was affiliated with the School of HPER.)

*EMMETT R. "BRANCH" MCCRACKEN, Professor in Physical Education for Men, stepped down as Head Basketball Coach at the close of the 1964–1965 season; however, he continued to teach and to serve the school in other capacities until his death in 1970.

JANET E. MCAULEY, Assistant Professor Emeritus of Physical Education for Women, retired August 1980.

*CHARLES MCDANIEL, Instructor in Physical Education for Men, died October 3, 1972, while in service to Indiana University.

JOHN M. MILLER, Professor of Kinesiology, retired March 1994.

ARTHUR D. MINDHEIM, Assistant Professor Emeritus of Kinesiology, retired June 1998.

ROBERT MORGAN, Lecturer of Kinesiology, retired May 2014.

HAROLD H. MORRIS, Professor Emeritus of Kinesiology, retired December 2003.

RICHARD F. MULL, Assistant Professor of Physical Education for Men, retired May 2007.

EDNA MUNRO, Professor Emeritus of Physical Education for Women, retired January 1961.

SAM NEWBERG, Assistant Professor Emeritus of Physical Education, retired December 1983.

JAMES W. "BILL" ORWIG, Professor Emeritus of Physical Education for Men, retired June 1976.

*MARJORIE P. PHILLIPS, Professor of Physical Education for Women, died in July 1961 while in service to Indiana University.

MARY LOUISE REMLEY, Professor Emeritus of Kinesiology, retired June 1996.

*ROBERT ROYER, Assistant Professor in Physical Education, died on December 5, 1957, while in service to Indiana University.

OTTO E. RYSER, Professor Emeritus of Physical Education, retired August 1981.

HILDA A. SHERWIN, Assistant Professor Emeritus of Kinesiology, retired May 1992.

ARTHUR T. SLATER-HAMMEL, Professor Emeritus of Physical Education, retired December 1978.

JAMES S. SKINNER, Professor Emeritus of Kinesiology, retired August 2005.

*FRAN SNYGG, Professor of Kinesiology, died on February 10, 1996, while in service to Indiana University.

CLINTON H. STRONG, Professor Emeritus of Kinesiology, retired August 1992.

*ROBERT L. STUMPNER was approved for a promotion to Associate Professor of Physical Education for Men effective July 1, 1968; however, he died on May 21, 1968, while in service to Indiana University.

DOROTHY DEAN SUMMERS, Associate Professor Emeritus of Physical Education, retired May 1980.

PAUL SURBURG, Professor Emeritus of Kinesiology, retired August 2001.

WYNN F. UPDYKE, Professor Emeritus of Kinesiology, retired June 1997.

MARKHAM C. WAKEFIELD, Associate Professor Emeritus of Physical Education for Men, retired July 1966.

JANET P. WALLACE, Professor Emeritus of Kinesiology, retired December 2013.

LOUIS C. WATSON, Associate Professor of Physical Education, retired August 1987.

JERRY DIANA WILKERSON, Professor Emeritus of Kinesiology, retired June 2011.

JERAD LEE YEAGLEY, Assistant Professor Emeritus of Kinesiology, retired December 2003.

DEPARTMENT OF RECREATION, PARK, AND TOURISM STUDIES

DAVID R. AUSTIN, Professor Emeritus of Recreation and Park Administration, retired May 2005.

HERBERT BRANTLEY, Professor Emeritus of Recreation and Park Administration, retired July 1994.

REYNOLD E. CARLSON, Professor Emeritus of Recreation, retired June 1972.

DAVID M. COMPTON, Professor Emeritus of Recreation, Park, and Tourism Studies and of Environmental Health, retired May 2011.

THEODORE R. DEPPE, Professor Emeritus of Recreation, retired May 1987.

GARRETT G. EPPLEY, Professor Emeritus of Recreation, retired July 1967.

BARBARA A. HAWKINS, Professor Emeritus of Recreation, Park, and Tourism Studies, retired May 2014.

BRUCE HRONEK, Professor Emeritus of Recreation, Park, and Tourism Studies, retired June 2010.

RICHARD W. LAWSON, Associate Professor Emeritus of Recreation and Park Administration, retired October 1992.

JANET R. MACLEAN, Professor Emeritus of Recreation, retired June 1982.

W. DONALD MARTIN, Associate Professor Emeritus of Recreation and Park Administration, retired May 1995.

JOEL F. MEIER, Professor Emeritus of Recreation and Park Administration, retired May 2007.

JAMES A. PETERSON, Professor Emeritus of Recreation, retired May 1990.

JAMES RIDENOUR, Professor Emeritus of Recreation and Park Administration, retired June 2001.

THOMAS J. RILLO, Professor Emeritus of Recreation and Park Administration, retired May 1992.

GARY M. ROBB, Associate Professor of Recreation and Park Administration, retired May 2008.

CRAIG M. ROSS, Professor Emeritus of Recreation, Park, and Tourism Studies, retired May 2014.

JOHN M. ROSS, Assistant Professor Emeritus of Recreation and Park Administration, retired June 1998.

RUTH VIRGINIA RUSSELL, Professor Emeritus of Recreation, Park, and Tourism Studies, retired July 2010.

GEORGE E. SCHLAFER, Assistant Professor Emeritus of Recreation, retired June 1950.

DANIEL RAY SHARPLESS, Academic Specialist Emeritus of Recreation, Park, and Tourism Studies, retired June 2010.

ROBERT W. TULLY, Professor Emeritus of Recreation and Park Administration, retired May 1976.

APPENDIX C. *Distinguished School and Alumni Awards*

HONORARY DOCTORATES AWARDED BY THE SCHOOL OF HPER

Indiana University awarded the following honorary degrees on behalf of the School of HPER:

Honorary Doctor of Humane Letters to Reynold Carlson, 1983 Commencement.

Honorary Doctor of Humane Letters to Richard "Dick" Enberg, 2002 Commencement.

Honorary Doctor of Science to John Seffrin, 2008 Winter Commencement.

HPER RECIPIENTS OF INDIANA UNIVERSITY DISTINGUISHED ALUMNI SERVICE AWARD

Fourteen alumni of the School of HPER/School of Public Health have been recipients of the IU Distinguished Alumni Service Award, the university's highest accolade reserved solely for alumni. The award recognizes outstanding achievements by alumni of Indiana University as demonstrated by their accomplishments in their chosen fields of endeavor and by their significant contributions benefiting the community, state, nation, or university.

(2013) Roderick Paige
(2012) Richard "Dick" Enberg
(2012) Curt Simic
(2008) Tony Mobley
(2006) George Taliaferro

(2005) Mildred Morgan Ball
(2003) Larry R. Ellis
(2000) Sandy Altman Knapp
(1998) Dale Stark Leff
(1993) Don A. Veller

(1989) Frank B. Jones
(1988) William S. Armstrong
(1987) Harrison B. Wilson, Jr.
(1960) Everett S. Dean

W. W. PATTY DISTINGUISHED ALUMNI AWARD

The W. W. Patty Distinguished Alumni Award is presented annually to graduates of the School of Public Health who have demonstrated outstanding personal and professional achievement. Since the award's inception in 1976, recipients have embodied the ideals set forth by Indiana University's first dean of the school that was formerly named Health, Physical Education, and Recreation, Willard W. Patty. Under his leadership, the school rose to national stature and produced some of the finest professionals in the fields of public health, recreation, and physical education.

RECIPIENTS

(2015) Richard Killingsworth
(2015) Michael Lysko
(2014) Gene Monahan
(2013) Dale W. Evans
(2013) George Taliaferro
(2012) William A. Oleckno
(2012) Curtis R. Simic, Sr.
(2011) Amy Eisenstein
(2011) Troy Vaughn
(2011) Roger Zabik
(2010) Jeffrey Clark
(2010) Fran Cleland Donnelly
(2010) Tony Mobley
(2009) Richard A. Crosby
(2009) J. Robert Rossman
(2009) Sue Willey
(2008) Roberta Ogletree
(2008) Jan Combs
(2008) Mick Renneisen
(2007) Thomas M. Davis
(2007) Margot E. Faught
(2007) Norman Merrifield
(2006) David McSwane
(2006) Tom Crawford
(2006) Eugene Young
(2005) Antoinette Gentile

(2005) Ronald A. Olson
(2005) Donald I. Wagner
(2004) William Considine
(2004) Bertha M. Cato
(2004) Susan J. Telljohann
(2003) Marilyn Looney
(2003) Guy Parcel
(2003) James Peterson
(2002) Beth Collins Pateman
(2002) Tommy Frederick
(2002) Sandra Little
(2001) Stephen Bender
(2001) Joan Hult
(2001) Charles Wilt
(2000) G. Daniel Howard
(2000) Andrew S. Jackson
(2000) Anne Binkley
(1998) Laura Kann
(1998) Michael G. Davis
(1998) Philip S. Rea
(1997) Robert Behnke
(1997) James Anderson
(1997) Louis Twardzik
(1996) Edward J. Koenemann
(1996) W. P. Buckner, Jr.
(1996) Brent Rushall

(1995) Morgan Pigg
(1995) Anthony Annarino
(1995) Richard J. Schroth
(1995) Daryl L. Siedentop
(1994) Betty van der Smissen
(1994) David Ng
(1993) Steven N. Blair
(1992) Robert H. Kirk
(1991) Phyllis M. Ford
(1990) Harold M. Barrow
(1989) Robert F. Toalson
(1988) Walter Paul Kroll
(1987) Warren E. Schaller
(1986) Richard "Dick" Enberg
(1985) Robert O. Yoho
(1984) Clifford T. Seymour
(1983) Jack E. Razor
(1982) Mark E. Dean
(1981) Fred E. Darling
(1980) Robert Warner Ruhe
(1979) Harry G. Fritz
(1978) Hester Beth Bland
(1977) Richard J. Tiernan
(1976) Raymond Struck

JOHN R. ENDWRIGHT ALUMNI SERVICE AWARD

Established in 1986, the John R. Endwright Alumni Service Award is an annual award that recognizes outstanding service and contributions to Indiana University and the school. The award is a reflection of former Dean John R. Endwright's commitment to maintaining strong ties between the school and its graduates. It was Endwright who, earlier in his career, as an assistant to Dean W. W. Patty, suggested that a school's foundation would only be as strong as the relationships it established with its alumni.

RECIPIENTS

(2015) Robert Nickovich
(2015) Mary Boutain
(2014) Scott Chakan
(2014) Tom Templin
(2013) Vicki Scott
(2012) Laura Newton
(2011) David R. Austin
(2011) Kele Ding
(2011) Melissa Heston
(2010) Nick DiGrino
(2010) Harrison B. Wilson
(2010) Andrew Kanu
(2009) Mark Wilson
(2009) Debra Wright Knapp
(2009) Jane H. Adams
(2008) Thomas Feldman
(2008) Suzanne Crouch
(2008) Kelly Powell
(2007) Russell Sinn
(2007) Elizabeth J. Monnier

(2007) Rin Seibert
(2006) Robert Lubitz
(2006) Tami Benham Deal
(2006) Peter Cunningham
(2005) David R. Hopkins
(2005) Wendy Z. Hultsman
(2005) Helen L. Scheibner
(2004) George Holland
(2004) John C. Ozmun
(2004) James Murphy
(2003) Steven Kintigh
(2003) Robert Synovitz
(2003) Peter Werner
(2002) James Garges
(2002) Elizabeth Majestic
(2002) Kenneth Mosely
(2001) Joy Miller Kirchner
(2001) George H. Oberle
(2001) Kenneth G. Stella
(2000) Hugh Jessop

(2000) Walt Bellamy
(2000) Lee Burton
 (posthumously)
(1998) C. Harold Veenker
(1998) Marian G. Miller
(1998) Sandy Knapp
(1997) Dean Kleinschmidt
(1997) Mildred Ball
(1997) Jane Boubel
(1996) William Brattain
(1996) Norma Jean Johnson
(1996) Anthony Pantaleoni
(1995) William Koch
 (posthumously)
(1995) Michael "Kent" Benson
(1995) Janet Seaman
(1995) Joseph Cindrich
(1992) Leroy Z. Compton
(1990) George T. Wilson
(1986) Sam Newberg

ANITA ALDRICH DISTINGUISHED ALUMNI AWARD

The Anita Aldrich Distinguished Alumni Award is presented annually to graduates who have demonstrated outstanding achievements in professional practice, service to the community, and loyalty to Indiana University as related to the advancement of girls and women in sports, fitness, and the pursuit of healthy lifestyles.

RECIPIENTS

(2015) Mary Schutten
(2014) Kathleen Cordes
(2013) Jerry Wilkerson
(2012) Sandy Searcy

(2011) Sage Steele
(2010) Judith Campbell
(2009) Joan S. Hult
(2008) Jeannine Butler

(2007) Peggy Martin
(2006) Barbara Gordon Filippell
(2005) Mildred Ball

TONY MOBLEY INTERNATIONAL DISTINGUISHED ALUMNI AWARD

The Tony Mobley International Distinguished Alumni Award, established in 2000, is presented annually to international graduates of the School of Public Health who have demonstrated outstanding personal and professional achievement. The award was named for Tony Mobley upon his retirement in 2002 after serving twenty-six years as Dean of the school, the longest-serving school dean in the history of Indiana University. Recipients demonstrate the ideals, leadership, and professionalism that helped to raise the school to national prominence under Mobley's leadership. This award reflects the growing stature of the school as a global leader.

RECIPIENTS

(2015) Robin Milhausen
(2014) Talal Hashim
(2013) Trevor Garrett
(2012) Dr. Chin-Hsung Kao
(2011) Laura Capranica
(2010) Frank Pyke

(2009) János Váczi
(2008) Chi-Huang "Mike"
    Huang
(2007) Zhiwei Pan
(2006) Nikos Stavropoulos
(2005) Vorasak Pienchob

(2004) Umit Kesim
(2003) Tepwanee Homsanit
(2002) Farouk Abdel-Wahab
(2001) Tsai Min-Chung
(2000) Jose Medalha

EARLY CAREER OUTSTANDING ALUMNI AWARD

The Early Career Outstanding Alumni Award is an annual recognition given to an alumnus of the School of Public Health at Indiana University who, through exceptional achievement, has distinguished himself/herself through professional accomplishment, community service, or service to the university.

RECIPIENTS

(2015) Sarah Beth Goldman
(2014) Kalen Irsay
(2013) Brittany Hollingsworth
(2012) Allison Chopra

Index

About the Authors

MOHAMMAD R. TORABI received a BS and MSPH from Tehran University, a PhD from Purdue University, and an MPH from Indiana University. Currently, he is Founding Dean of the School of Public Health–Bloomington and serves as Co-Director of the Rural Center for AIDS/STD Prevention. He has extensively published his research in a variety of major national and international journals in the field of public health. Notably, his research in the areas of tobacco as a gateway drug and tobacco policy has made an impact at national and international levels. Professor Torabi has served as a research consultant for various state and national organizations, including governmental and nongovernmental agencies, and has presented his research at major national and international conferences.

Professor Torabi serves as Editor of the *Health Education Monograph Series* and formerly served as Assistant Research Editor of the *Journal of School Health* and as a research editor for the *American Journal of Health Behavior*. He is a former president of the American Academy of Health Behavior. He has served as a member of the National Executive Board of the American School Health Association, as an at-large member of the National Council of the American Lung Association, as a board member of the American Association of Health Education, and as a member of the National Executive Committee of the Eta Sigma Gamma, a Health Science Honorary. He served as Vice President for the North American Region office of the International Union of Health Promotion and Education. as the President of the American Lung Association of Indiana, and as President of the IU Chapter of Phi Delta Kappa. Currently, he is the Health Education Commissioner for the International Council for Health, Physical Education, and Recreation. He holds a gubernatorial appointment on the Executive Board, Tobacco Prevention and Cessation. Professor Torabi's accomplishments have been recognized with numerous awards, which are noted in his biography in chapter 5.

Courtesy of IU School of Public Health–Bloomington.

Photograph by Garrett J. Poortinga, Green Hat Media LLC, 2015. Used by permission.

BARBARA A. HAWKINS is Professor Emeritus of Recreation, Park, and Tourism Studies. She joined the Developmental Training Center as Program Coordinator for Early Childhood at Indiana University in 1981. Previously, she was an assistant professor at the University of Maine. During her early work at IU, she founded and directed the Program on Aging and Developmental Disabilities, one of the first of its kind in the country. Her ten-year longitudinal study of aging-related change in older adults with intellectual disabilities provided first-of-its-kind evidence about behavioral and cognitive changes in aging adults with Down syndrome as precursors to decline with early-onset Alzheimer's dementia.

In addition to her departmental responsibilities, Dr. Hawkins served as Director of the IU Center on Aging and Aged. Her research at the center focused on the health, daily-life activities, and well-being of nondisabled older adults. She was nationally and internationally recognized for her work in the area of aging well. She secured more than $2 million in external funding to support her research and creative activities during her career at Indiana University.

Professor Hawkins is the author of more than 150 publications, as well as instructional videotapes and three assessment tools, *Five Dimensional Life Satisfaction Index* (1997, 2nd edition), *Leisure Assessment Inventory* (2002), and *Designing Environments for Active Living* (2012). She is the author or coauthor of more than fifty books, chapters, and technical reports. Her most recent textbook is *Active Living in Older Adulthood: Principles and Practices of Activity Programs* (2009).

Professor Hawkins is a Fellow of the Association for Gerontology in Higher Education and of the Academy of Leisure Sciences. Among her honors are the Society of Park and Recreation Presidential Citation for Leadership Service; the 2004 School of HPER Outstanding Researcher Award; the Presidential Award and Citation for Outstanding Service from the National Therapeutic Recreation Society; a Fellowship in the CIC Academic Leadership Program; and the Innovations in Aging Award from the Leisure and Aging Section, NRPA. In 2014, she was the recipient of the Distinguished Leadership Award from the IU School of Public Health–Bloomington.

Courtesy of IU School of Public Health–Bloomington.

DAVID M. SKIRVIN serves as Assistant Dean for Administration at the Indiana University School of Public Health–Bloomington. He received three degrees from Indiana University: the BA degree in 1982, the MS degree in 1986, and the EdD degree in Higher Education Administration in 1998. He also earned a Certificate in Public Management from the Indiana University School of Public and Environmental Affairs in 1989. His occupational interests lie primarily in the areas of university operational management, including budgetary and personnel administration, and facility management. His teaching focuses on finance and budget issues that affect health, sport, and leisure-related organizations.